The Wind Cries Mary

Murders That Shook A Power Town

ERIKA GREY

Pe Danté Press
Danbury, CT

Pe Danté Press

The Wind Cries Mary: Murders That Shook A Power Town
Copyright © 2009 by Erika Grey
All rights reserved. No part of this publication may be reproduced
in any form without written permission from PeDante Press™

PeDante Press™
Suite #4 White Oak
Danbury CT 06810

Library of Congress Control Number: 2009939462
Grey, Erika.
  The Wind Cries Mary : Murders That Shook a Power Town / Erika Grey
    p.   cm.
  Includes bibliographical references (p. 163-170)
  ISBN 978-0-9790199-1-3
  ISBN 0-9790199-1-5

Printed in the United States of America

This book is dedicated to the memory of the victims and their families and to my own family for their support and encouragement in writing this book.

Also by Erika Grey
The Seat of the Antichrist: Bible Prophecy and the European Union

CONTENTS

Chapter 1: The Disappearance of Mary Mount 7

Chapter 2: The Search 23

Chapter 3: A Sad Discovery 39

Chapter 4: Riders on The Storm 53

Chapter 5: The Rice Murders 69

Chapter 6: The Search For John Rice 85

Chapter 7: The Trial 95

Chapter 8: The Rice Household 107

Chapter 9: A Rice-Mount Connection 117

Chapter 10: John Rice Freed 127

Chapter 11: Cured? Rehabilitated? 137

Chapter 12: The Wind Cries Mary 147

Epilogue 155

Photos 159

Bibliography 163

CHAPTER ONE

THE DISAPPEARANCE OF MARY MOUNT

No one ever thought it could ever happen in Connecticut's "Next Station to Heaven," a name given to the town of New Canaan because of its stately homes in picturesque settings. In the 1960s, major crimes in New Canaan, Connecticut were unheard of. Shortly after World War II, a woman shot and killed her lover, and the act achieved status as New Canaan's crime of the century. This changed in 1969 and 1970 when New Canaan, a relatively safe town by today's standards, experienced in those years both serial and mass murder.

Serial and mass murders generally do not occur in "power towns," towns in which a high percentage of the residents are listed in the "Who's Who" directories. Within Fairfield County, Connecticut exist three of the seven power towns listed for the entire United States: Greenwich, Darien, and New Canaan. Bedford, New York makes four of the seven located in close proximity to one another.

The *raison d'être* for these towns being so close to one another is because of their close proximity to New York City. These towns act as "bedroom communities" for many executives who commute to New York. With New York being home to many corporate headquarters; major television networks; and Wall Street, as well a capital for fashion, the arts, and theater, Fairfield County, Connecticut and Westchester County, New York enjoy status as suburbs for the most powerful people in these industries.

Connecticut offers "the country" for those who do not desire the fast-paced, apartment lifestyle of New York.

Greenwich, the first town one enters after leaving New York, has earned the title of Connecticut's – and the nation's – wealthiest community. New Canaan ranks just behind Greenwich in wealth and status.

When one enters New Canaan, one of the first things one notices, besides stately, well-landscaped homes, is the number of Mercedes, BMWs, Jaguars, stretch limousines and other expensive cars on the road, which outnumber those in the mid- to lower-price ranges. For those who have ascended to high-status positions, New Canaan is the ultimate destination, while the working class tends to view this wealthy community as being out of touch with the real world.

In the mid to late 1960s, New Canaan never suffered any of the problems that other cities in Connecticut experienced. Violent crime in New Canaan was virtually non-existent. While race wars raged within inner-city high schools, New Canaan's schools boasted that 85% of its graduates were college bound.

Many high-powered individuals and their families have come and gone since 1969 and 1970 but those who lived during those years still talk about the events that took place and hit their gas pedals a little harder each time they drive by one of the crime scenes. Although more than 40 years have passed, those who lived in New Canaan when these crimes occurred still find them no less shocking.

In the late 1960s, 14,000 people lived in New Canaan and enjoyed its bucolic setting and outstanding schools. The latter was the major factor in Joseph Mount's decision to move his wife Lily and their four school-age children from Texas to New Canaan when IBM transferred him to its White Plains, New York headquarters in 1967. IBM had promoted Dr. Mount to Scientific Center Manager, and with the promotion came the move to Connecticut.

The Wind Cries Mary

Joseph Mount had a Ph.D. in mathematics and he specialized in numerical analysis, the study of the computational aspects of calculus. Unlike Dr. Mount's peers in New Canaan, who had attended the same Ivy League colleges as their fathers, Dr. Mount's father had worked as a carpenter in Memphis, Tennessee. Joseph Mount attended UCLA on the GI bill and went on to complete the highest level of education of anyone in his family; he also achieved the most financially.

Joseph Mount enjoyed a happy marriage with his wife Lily, whom he had met at UCLA. Lily was born in Los Angeles, California to a Japanese father and a German mother. Unfortunately, because of her father's nationality, she was forced to spend some of her childhood years in a Japanese detention camp during World War II. Despite those early years of hardship, Lily grew into a gracious, intelligent woman.

Once married, the Mounts moved to Alabama where Dr. Mount began a teaching career as a professor of biomathematics at the University of Alabama. while in Alabama, Joseph and Lily started their family. Joseph Jr. was the first born. David followed. Lily's third pregnancy produced another boy, William. On April 14, 1959, the Mounts reveled when Lily gave birth to a hoped-for baby girl. They named her Mary Katherine. The Mount boys doted on their baby sister. Billy, closest in age to Mary, saw in her a constant playmate.

In 1960, Joseph went to work for IBM and the Mount family moved to Houston, Texas, where Joseph also took a job as an associate professor at Baylor University. There at Baylor Medical Center, Joseph Mount worked with the world-famous physician, surgeon, pioneer of heart surgery, and medical statesman, Dr. Michael Debakey who, in 1969, received the highest honor a United States citizen can receive, the Presidential Medal of Freedom and Distinction. In 1987, President Ronald Reagan awarded Debakey the National Medal of Science. Although Joseph Mount held a managerial job at IBM, applications of computers in medicine interested him throughout his life and it was in this area that he assisted Dr. Debakey.

Along with his mathematical acumen, Joseph was very religious, choosing a church for his family based on the personality of the minister and the overall atmosphere at the church. While in Texas, the Mount family attended Sunday services regularly.

The Mounts were firmly settled in Texas when, in 1967, IBM offered to promote Joseph to Scientific Center Manager. The position required that he move close to the White Plains, New York headquarters. Joseph attempted to make the transition as smooth as possible for his family and, after researching the area, he discovered that New Canaan, Connecticut, a small, affluent community in the southwestern portion of the state, was home to many New York City and IBM executives. Dubbed by its local newspaper, "the next station to heaven," New Canaan offered beautiful estate homes, country clubs, numerous activities and a high school where the vast majority of its students went on to college. Joseph Mount was moving up in the world, and he wanted his children amongst those whose fathers had graduated from the nation's most reputable colleges and held high-paying jobs in Fortune 500 companies.

Once in New Canaan, the Mounts immediately joined a church, so as not to upset the family's routine of church on Sunday. The children were enrolled in various activities. Mary attended Girl Scouts while the boys went into the Boy Scouts.

Initially, the Mounts rented a home on Millport Avenue. Though not considered a prominent part of town, the charming house had ample room to accommodate the Mounts' four children. While living on Millport Avenue, Joseph and Lily worked with a builder to design their new home in New Canaan. The architectural drawings rested continuously on the dining room table while the Mounts negotiated with the builder as to the design and layout of the house.

On January 13, 1969, the Mounts moved to their new house on 45 Willowbrook Road. They purchased it for $80,000. Though that was considered a good deal of money in 1969, the Mounts enjoyed upper middle income status and not the great wealth of those who inhabited the town's outskirts. Their new home, located less than a mile from their residence on Millport, was located on a cul de sac and provided spacious room for the four children.

At the time of the move, Joseph was 16, David was 13, Billy was 12 and Mary looked forward to her 10th birthday in April. In the rear of the house beyond the back yard, stood a 15-acre preserve known as Kiwanis Park, which contained a large, man-made swimming hole with sand spread around it to make it seem like a beach. To the back of the pond, a large green shed stood to the right of a basketball court. A snack bar, rest rooms, and a caretaker's home, all attached to one another, were to the right of the pond. Opposite the snack bar area, on the other side of the pond a wooden "Kiwanis Park" sign rested on a hill amidst shrubbery. The neighborhood homes, including that of the Mounts, could be seen through the trees that surrounded the entire swimming area of the park. The Mount's home was located to the rear of the wooded area behind the green shed.

From the back of Kiwanis Park, one could not see all the way to the front of the park. To get to the front you had to drive in from Old Norwalk Road. From that road, one could see a small nursery school, a sandbox and swing set. Behind the school, a wall of trees blocked one's view to the rest of Kiwanis Park. A stranger driving down Old Norwalk Road would have assumed that the nursery and playthings outside of the school were all that Kiwanis Park offered. It wasn't until one drove past the wall of trees that one discovered the park extended to include a swimming hole.

For Mary, 1969 held more memories than previous times because she was excited about moving into the new home. On April 14, Mary turned 10 and, although there were no children her age who lived on her street, she considered herself lucky to have a park situated practically in her back yard. Every spring, the town spread new sand around the swimming hole. In preparation for this, town trucks had dumped a huge pile of sand at the back of the pool, not far from Mary's house. To Mary and Billy this sandpile was a child's paradise. David often went to the park alone and played at the basketball court, while Billy and Mary tended to go together. When the weather permitted, the Mount children played in the park as often as possible.

Mary was described by young boys her age as a pretty girl, with blue eyes and a shining smile that stood out against her brown shoulder-length hair. Mary's schoolmates viewed her as friendly, quiet and fun to be with. She had been known to jump into a game of marbles with the boys. Mary's homeroom teacher considered her very intelligent and her consistent A and B grades delighted her parents. Her role as peacemaker in other children's disputes was also apparent. Since she had three older brothers who would engage in many small quarrels, Mary often helped to negotiate and put an end to conflicts. So adept was she at this skill that even in grade school she was able to sense when a conflict of interests was in progress and help resolve the disagreement.

Tuesday, May 27, 1969 brought sunshine and hence a great day for going to play at the park. Nearly all of the trees had bloomed and the feeling of the approaching summer filled the air, along with the anticipation of the joy felt at the end of another school year. Mary and Billy came home from school and, after finishing a snack and completing their homework, decided to go out and play in the huge sandpile, which would only remain a few weeks before it would be spread on the ground to serve as a beach. Around 4:30 p.m. Lily, Mary and Billy were all home together. David was at the YMCA, while Joe, Mary's oldest brother, was at the high school.

Mary and Billy walked through their back yard to Kiwanis Park. Although only a few short months earlier, Mary could look through bare trees and see the park from her back yard, the blooming of all of the trees acted as a barrier between her home and the park. Mary and Billy took the short walk through patchy woods and swamp to get to the sandpile.

The family cat, Geezo, followed them, as was his habit. Everywhere that Mary went, Geezo followed. All three settled near the sandpile and remained there, playing. The spectacle caused Mrs. Cogswell, the wife of the caretaker, to take notice. The Cogswells lived in the caretaker's home adjacent to the snack bars and rest rooms. The sandpile could be seen from the Cogswell's kitchen window. At around 6 o'clock, Mrs. Cogswell's 21-year-old daughter, Georgia, went out to the sandpile to play with Geezo. Mrs. Cogswell, who owned cats but had never seen a cat who followed his owners everywhere, followed shortly behind Georgia and walked over to Mary and Billy. She couldn't get over how the cat tagged along with Mary everywhere she went.

Mrs. Cogswell chatted with the children for a few minutes, until Billy told Mrs. Cogswell and Mary that he had to go home to get ready for a Boy Scout meeting. Mrs. Cogswell and Georgia decided to go home as well, since Mrs. Cogswell had to continue preparing dinner for her husband. Mary and Billy both ran to the top of the sandpile and down again. When they got to the bottom, they both put their shoes back on.

Billy looked at his watch; it read 6:23. He said to Mary, "I've got to go; let's go." Mary told Bill that she would be right along. When Billy returned home, Lily asked him where Mary was. He told her that Mary would be home in a few minutes. Lily told Billy that she had some muffins in the oven and, if the timer went off, he should take them out. She was leaving to pick up David from the YMCA. Bill went upstairs to take a shower and get dressed for his Boy Scout meeting.

At the same time, Mrs. Cogswell noticed it was 6:35 p.m. and she told her daughter Georgia to call police headquarters to see if Mr. Cogswell had left for home. While Mrs. Cogswell was in the kitchen, she noticed a car driving up the driveway in front of her cottage. It passed her kitchen window and headed for the sandpile area. There was an orange Town of New Canaan truck, used to dredge the pool, parked in the area in front of this window, obstructing Mrs. Cogswell's view of the car. Georgia, who was in her bedroom when her mother asked her to make the phone call, noticed a white car as it passed her bedroom window and drove in the direction of the sand pile. In the car was a dark-haired white male, wearing a light-colored shirt.

Mrs. Cogswell assumed it was the man who came regularly to check the pump, although she did not know what type of vehicle the pump man drove. After a few minutes, she noticed the car drive out of the driveway, alongside her kitchen window, and head out of the park. She didn't see anyone in the vehicle other than the operator, who appeared to be driving normally. The car moved slowly on its way in and out of Kiwanis Park. Mrs. Cogswell didn't think twice about the car because the new houses that had been recently built in the neighborhood had been generating greater traffic through the park.

Not every car that drove into Kiwanis Park had access to the pool area. Drivers had to turn around in a grassy meadow that acted as a parking lot, which Mrs. Cogswell viewed from a distance through her living room window. A stockade fence cubicle outside the kitchen door, which hid garden implements, garbage, and a clothesline partly blocked the view.

Mr. Cogswell arrived home at 6:40 and the footprints that remained on the sandpile bore witness to the fun and laughter experienced by Mary and Billy a half hour earlier.

When Lily Mount arrived home at 6:42, Billy had finished his shower and the muffins were still baking, but Mary had not yet returned. Lily put dinner on the table for herself, David, Billy, and Mary. Billy didn't want to eat. At 7:00, Lily called out for Mary, but received no response. She told Billy to go back to Kiwanis Park, find Mary, and tell her it was dinner time. Billy walked barefoot back to the park, but didn't see Mary anywhere; there was only a man with a metal detector looking for coins by the pool. He returned home and told his mother that Mary was not there. This news alarmed Lily, who had David call out for Mary.

David called and called, thinking that Mary might be somewhere around the yard, but his cries were met with silence. Lily became more concerned, but felt that somehow Billy may have missed her, so she decided to go and look herself.

Around 7:30, Lily and Billy walked over to Kiwanis Park. Billy showed her the area they had played in and pointed to the spot where he last saw Mary. They checked around the sandpile, and noticed a man on the east side of the pool still trying to detect coins. At around a quarter to eight, they returned home because it was time for Billy to be taken to Boy Scouts. As they were leaving the park, Billy thought he heard Mary's voice. Lily hoped that Mary might be at home and somehow they had missed her. Maybe the voice was Mary playing in their yard.

When Lily and Billy arrived back home, however, Mary was not there. Lily, in a state of increasing anxiety, thought Mary might still be somewhere at the park. She drove Billy to his Boy Scout meeting, giving great thought to Mary's whereabouts. After she dropped Billy off, she drove back through Kiwanis Park, but didn't see any sign of Mary. She drove home, parked her car and walked back to the park. She stopped and asked the man with the metal detector if he had seen Mary. She also saw two little boys and asked them if they had seen Mary. Nobody had. Lily returned home in a panic. Besides Mary's apparent intelligence, Lily considered her to be an obedient girl. Mary had never returned home late. Even when Mary took a stroll with Geezo every afternoon, she was never late returning home.

Lily and David frantically searched the area for Mary. The sun was beginning to go down and the day's sunshine was being replaced by the gray sky that was the predecessor of darkness. With it, gloom and uncertainty filled the air. Kiwanis Park didn't bear its normal quietude, but rather, a chilling silence.

Dr. Joseph Mount enjoyed teaching and volunteered his time at Norwalk Community College two nights a week to teach data processing to minority students. He was scheduled to tutor a couple of students that evening and, when they arrived, Lily and David were in the middle of their search. They told the students what was going on and told them to notify Joseph Mount once he arrived home if they were not back. While Lily and David were searching for Mary, Joseph Mount arrived home. The two students who were waiting for him told him that Mary was missing and Lily and David were looking for her. Within minutes, Lily and David returned home. Mary was still nowhere to be found.

Joseph asked if Lily and David had checked at the caretaker's home and they said "no." The family now turned to the hope that Mary might have gone to the Cogswells' and lost track of time. Joseph arrived at Mrs. Cogswell's door at about 8:15 and asked if she had seen Mary. Mrs. Cogswell told him about the white car that had passed her house in the 15 minutes between the time she returned from talking with Mary and the time her husband returned for supper.

Mrs. Cogswell went out with Joseph to look for Mary and found Mary's kitten at the east side of the pool, near the bushes.

Joseph returned home and, at 8:25, he telephoned the New Canaan Police to report Mary missing. Captain Corsen and six other officers arrived at the Mount home and learned that Mary had been missing since approximately 6:30.

Missing children calls were not uncommon at the New Canaan Police Department. They were reported somewhat routinely but, in all of the cases, the child was soon found after the police arrived. In one instance, as the police were searching the yard of a missing child's home, the child – who had been hiding in a tree – jumped onto a police officer and bit him. When the police arrived at the Mount home, they assumed this was another case where the child would simply turn up.

Captain Corsen and his men conducted a search of the immediate area of Kiwanis Park and the Mount home, but Mary did not turn up. Lily went to pick up Billy from the Boy Scouts at 9 o'clock and informed him that they still hadn't found Mary and had called the police. When she returned home, she made many telephone calls to Mary's friends, but no one knew of her whereabouts. There was a slim hope that the man in the white car might have been a parent of one of Mary's friends. Lily made the calls and all of them proved fruitless. Mary was not at friend's house.

At 9:15, the New Canaan police launched a search. For the first time since the great flood of 1955, the 7-7-7 signal sounded on the firehouse horn, summoning all off-duty policemen and auxiliary police. New Canaan Police Chief Keller contacted Lieutenant Ralph Scott, Chief Detective, who was in New York City that evening.

Ralph Scott was considered a good officer, well liked by many in the department. Although New Canaan had become home to many transients, there was a core group of residents who had lived there most of their lives. Ralph was among this group. He'd lived in New Canaan from the time he was five years old, when his family moved from nearby Vista, New York. He graduated from New Canaan High School in 1951 and, while many of his classmates went on to colleges and universities, Ralph went into the Marines, where he served for three years. After the Marines, Ralph enrolled at the University of Bridgeport, but he felt that he had been out of school too long to get back into a scholarly mode, so he dropped out. At that time, a job became available at the New Canaan Police Department. Ralph had friends in the department who talked him into taking the job; he was hired in May 1956.

Although Ralph felt reluctant about joining the force, he found that he really enjoyed police work. In 1963, after seven years of service on the force, Ralph earned the rank of detective. From there he was promoted to Sergeant Detective and then to Lieutenant, a position that carried the responsibility of overseeing all the other detectives.

Until the Mount case, Ralph had handled mostly burglaries, of which the area had its share because of its affluence. Drug addicts who lived in the surrounding cities committed most of the robberies. Ralph was wise to the county's troublemakers and criminal activities. The Mary Mount case would become the crime that disturbed him more than any other case he had worked on.

Chief Keller was upset about Lieutenant Scott's initial absence because this case was not a usual one for New Canaan. Although missing children's cases were somewhat common, this incident from the start had indications of being serious because of the circumstances. Mary told her brother she would be home in a few minutes and she was never late. The white car that entered the area in which Mary was last seen playing was not a good sign either. The area was also surrounded by small ponds – Mary might have fallen into one and might be injured or have even drowned. Things did not look good.

For the Mounts, each hour of darkness that passed brought greater horror. At midnight, when there was still no word from Mary, the Mounts entered the beginning of another day of anguish. Each time they looked to Mary's empty room, the reality of her disappearance burned in their hearts. The unbearable pain left them in an emotional state of shock. Joseph Mount was determined to shield his wife and sons from as much of the horror as he could. For their sake, he tried to keep the family functioning as normally as possible, and they did, but not without each of them carrying around the tormenting question of what could possibly have happened to Mary.

At 5:15 Wednesday morning, Chief Keller called out over 100 off-duty policemen and volunteer firemen, who conducted a detailed search from the Mount home, through Kiwanis Park, to the road which housed the park. Lieutenant Ralph Scott arrived early that morning. During the search, Don Hersam, both publisher of the New Canaan Advertiser and Fire Chief, suggested to the Chief and detectives to report Mary's disappearance in the public media on the chance that she and her abductor might be seen. There were no media representatives out at this early hour and Mr. Hersam advised they notify the area dailies and radio outlets.

Billy's classmate and neighbor, 12-year-old Chuck Carrol, joined the search. At 6:30 a.m., he discovered Mary's left brown loafer. Ralph Scott asked Chuck to show him the exact spot where the loafer was found, and he searched the area for tire marks, a sign of a scuffle or any other evidence, but found none. The abductor's tire tracks were among many sets of tracks left by town trucks that had been to the pool area. Chuck found the loafer in the grass in the direction of Mary's house as if she started walking away from the sand pile toward her home.

Detective Scott interviewed Billy, the Cogswell women and the man with the metal detector who'd been seen there the night before. He told police that he had arrived at the park at seven o'clock to look for coins. When he arrived, he didn't see any girl at the sand pile or any vehicles. At exactly 7:30, he remembered seeing a white car with a loud muffler drive in the area of the snack bar, and the next time he looked up it was driving away.

Taking into consideration the position Joseph Mount held with IBM, Detective Scott telephoned the FBI office in New Haven regarding the possibility that someone had kidnapped Mary Mount. Five FBI agents arrived at the New Canaan Police Department to assist in the investigation.

The police phoned Mary's grade school and spoke with her teacher, who confirmed that Mary had gotten on the bus to go home on Tuesday, the day of the disappearance. The teacher was in shock at hearing the news and it didn't take long for word to travel around town. Things like this didn't happen in New Canaan. The entire school went into a state of shock. All of the New York and

Fairfield County papers posted Mary's picture, along with the story of her disappearance.

On Wednesday, while Detective Ralph Scott searched for suspects, the area's four ponds located on private property were searched by divers. Water in the ponds ranged from 10 to 15 feet deep. "Visibility is about a foot, we'll have to feel our way around," yelled one of the divers as he entered a small, muddy pond. Police drained the ponds three times and found nothing. It was unlikely that Mary would have been found in one of the ponds, since her discarded loafer was found more than 1,000 yards from the nearest pond.

A bulldozer pushed apart the huge sandpile in the event that Mary had dug a tunnel that had collapsed. Members of the New Canaan Public Works Department sifted the sandpile for four hours. Police, firemen and volunteers covered the woodland in the area almost inch by inch. The FBI, State Police and State Police bloodhounds joined the search. Police headquarters had extra telephone services installed and police officials made calls all over the country seeking information and checking out tips. Thick files of mug shots and other data on known sex offenders were checked and rechecked along with examinations of long lists of car registrations. Police also issued a 13-state alarm.

On a tack board behind the desk where FBI agents worked hung a group of aerial photographs, mostly of the Kiwanis Park area, for constant and ready reference. Chief Keller felt that Mary was no longer in New Canaan.

By 7:00 p.m. on Wednesday, Mary had been missing for 24 hours. Police and volunteer firemen searched until 2:30 a.m. Bloodhounds from the Connecticut State Police Barracks in Bethany continued to search. All local homes were checked.

Based upon the finding of Mary's shoe, police theorized that someone had abducted Mary from the park. Police officers stated that children often leave sweaters and other articles of clothing behind and walk away, but shoes are rarely left behind by accident; when a child drops a shoe, he or she normally puts it right back on again. Police believed Mary lost the shoe when an abductor snatched her. Chief Keller told reporters he believed it was unlikely that Mary wandered off, but thought that her disappearance was due to some sort of perverted action; they believed that someone had picked her up in a car. Chief Keller suspected kidnapping for a number of reasons: "This young girl was very reliable and intelligent; she seemed to love her parents and had no reason to want to run away. She got along very well with her brothers. And then, we never have runaways here at the age of ten." Joseph Mount told police that Mary was very meticulous about her belongings and she wouldn't have left her shoe behind. They also doubted that Mary would take a ride from a stranger, but she might be friendly to someone who took a liking to her cat.

Joseph and Lily waited by the phone day and night. The polite, gracious Dr. Mount wouldn't answer any questions from reporters, for fear of saying the wrong thing in case Mary had indeed been kidnapped. He and his family were not even contacting friends or relatives for fear that they might miss an incoming call. With the police and FBI considering the possibility that a kidnapper snatched Mary for a ransom, the Mounts held on to the hope that Mary was still alive.

CHAPTER TWO

THE SEARCH

On Thursday, May 29, Joseph Mount went onto radio and television stations to make pleas for the safe return of Mary, to whom he referred to as "a truly wonderful child." He assured viewers and listeners that the FBI and police were not monitoring his telephone. He asked anyone with information to call him or any New Canaan resident, or any church or synagogue in the area. A newspaper covering the story even offered to relay any information to the Mount family through its answering service or staff members and assured that no calls would be monitored and confidences would be protected.

Joseph Mount made an appeal over WSTC radio station early Thursday morning and pleaded:

"This is Mary Mount's father speaking. At about 6:30 p.m. Tuesday our daughter Mary disappeared from Kiwanis Park in New Canaan. The anxiety and distress being experienced by our family as a result of her disappearance is beyond description. However, the most important factor in our life today is Mary's safety. For this reason we are making the following urgent plea:

If anyone listening to this broadcast knows our Mary is safe please indicate this fact to us in any manner you see fit, Some possibilities would be:

1. Contact us at 203-966-5346. This line will not be monitored.

2. Contact any church, synagogue, or public office and ask them to communicate the message to us.
3. Contact any resident of New Canaan and request that they communicate this information to us at 203-966-5346.

We emphasize two points:

1. Mary's safety is our only concern.
2. The proposed methods of communication are simply suggestions; the important point is we would like to know Mary is safe.

After receipt of any message we will be prepared to do anything in our power to assure Mary's safety."

Meanwhile, calls started to come in from several girls who said that a man in a white car had approached them near the park the same day that Mary had disappeared. One girl even got the man's license plate number. Police checked the registration and found that the car belonged to a construction worker who worked in the area. He became the police's first suspect. He allowed the police to search his vehicle and admitted to attempting to pick up high school girls in the area but he said that the most he had ever done was to kiss one of them. He had a very good alibi for Tuesday night. He had been at his insurance agent's office and then was at home for the rest of the evening.

A couple of other girls reported to police that they had been walking a couple of blocks from the park at about five o'clock on the day of Mary's disappearance, and a man had pulled over to ask if they wanted a ride. This man didn't match the description of the construction worker, and he drove an older model car. Thus the picture of a second suspect began to emerge.

On Thursday, beginning at 8:00 a.m., two police officers and two FBI agents conducted a search for Mary in the wooded area surrounding Kiwanis Park. They searched until 4 o'clock but found nothing relevant to the case. During this search, the construction worker walked into police headquarters, where Detective Ralph

Scott interviewed him and gave him a polygraph test after he denied any knowledge of Mary's disappearance. He did admit to trying to pick up girls in New Canaan but stated that he never molested them. He also admitted to molesting his sister when she was 16 years old.

Ralph Scott continued to interview possible suspects that day. The suspects varied from a motorcycle thief who had photographs of several young children in his possession to a 69-year-old deaf-mute whose friendliness toward young girls caused someone to phone the police and report him. Immediately after these interviews, Ralph Scott and another officer went to the home of a New Canaan resident who had a past history involving sex offenses but his mother established an alibi for him during the time of Mary Mount's disappearance on Tuesday night.

At five o'clock, police officers, members of the fire department, and 125 additional volunteers conducted a shoulder-to-shoulder search of the wooded areas on either side of the park. Police instructed the searchers to look for clothing, a shallow grave and, of course, Mary's body. A full description of her clothing was announced over the PA system. At nine o'clock that evening the futile search ended.

Late that night, the Norwalk police phoned Ralph Scott to tell him that a priest phoned to say that a man who sounded as if were in a hurry phoned his parish and said, "Listen carefully, tell the father of the girl, Mary, Mary is all right, not to worry about her, she is on the Long Island Sound." Then the caller hung up. Detective Scott immediately phoned Joseph Mount, and gave him the information, warning him that this could be a crank call.

With the nationally-televised news of Mary's disappearance, the Mount's former minister in Texas, upon hearing the news, drove to be with the family in New Canaan. Chief Keller sadly stated, "I have just the far-out hope that if Mary was taken away by a sex deviant, he drove her to some hideout where she may be alive. A hope," he said, "but not much of one."

By late Thursday, Joseph Mount had become very anxious and refused to answer most questions concerning Mary's disappearance except to say, "I'm scared to death. I don't know what to say." Adding to his anxiety and distress were four phone calls in which the caller had hung up every time.

By Friday, May 30, Detective Ralph Scott conducted interviews with many girls who told the police of their encounters with men in white cars, and he showed them photos of suspects. Nothing conclusive turned up. Within minutes after these fruitless interviews, a call came in that made Detective Scott hopeful that the case might get a break. A Mrs. Beloved phoned to say that at 4:30 on May 27, the day of the disappearance, she had been at Kiwanis Park with her two children when a car drove in and a man got out of it. When he saw Mrs. Beloved, he immediately turned around and got in his vehicle. He was a white male in his thirties, 5'6," 165-170 lbs., wearing khaki pants and a light plaid shirt.

Later that day, the Mounts' phone rang. On the other end a man told Lily Mount that a small girl who fit Mary's description was with two African-American males, both junkies, at 1945 McCarter Highway, North Newark, New Jersey. The caller believed Mary might be in a vacant apartment on the fourth floor at that address. Lily asked him his name, which he refused to give because he was afraid of what the two men might do to him if they found out he had called.

Ralph Scott phoned the Lieutenant of the Newark Police Department and requested that they check the address Lily had been given. The Mounts waited impatiently and hoped this call might bring an end to their horror, and return Mary to them. Joseph's mind raced with thoughts of what Mary's life could possibly be like while in the custody of these men. The Lieutenant sent his men and found nothing. Joseph Mount felt devastated by this crank call.

The evening news that night included a broadcast about the disappearance of Mary Mount. They provided the Mount's telephone number in case anyone had any information. Even concerned children telephoned. One 11-year-old girl phoned and hung up. A nine-year-old boy, one of Mary's classmates, did not want to believe that his friend had disappeared. When a very composed Mrs. Mount answered the phone, he asked if he could speak to Mary. When Lily said no, and asked why he had phoned, he said that he and Mary were going to trade some marbles. The two of them hung up sadly.

Early Saturday morning at 1:36, Joseph Mount received a call from an unidentified male who told him, "Mary is dead. Her body will be delivered up for $250,000. If not, by the time I call you again, the price will go up, or another member of your family is next. This is definitely not a call to play around with. I will call you back." The caller hung up. Joseph got the operator to trace the call to a coin box at the entrance to Grand Central Station in New York City. Police notified Ralph Scott who at once placed a call to the New York City Police Department, who made a call to the New York City FBI office. The FBI checked out the phone booth: the last one in a row of eight booths at that location. No results were obtained. The call, which threw Joseph Mount into a state of hysteria, ushered in Memorial Day, a holiday the Mounts would spend the rest of their lives trying to forget.

The hope that Mary had been kidnapped was fading, as no one had called for a ransom. The idea that a sex deviant had abducted Mary became the more likely scenario. The town police, state police and FBI continued to scour the area but did not come up with one clue. An observation plane was even sent out. Chief Keller expressed fear for Mary's life. "Every day that goes by lessens the chance she's alive," he said. "This looks like the work of a deviant, not someone looking for money. Whoever abducted Mary Mount is a pretty sick guy. We've covered the area five times over with men shoulder to shoulder; she's not in the area." Police dogs were unable to find a scent.

Police started going door-to-door in the Mounts' neighborhood in search of information. One of the police sergeants and a town worker sifted the piles of dirt located in the swamp area south of the park, in an effort to find anything that would be of significance to the investigation. Nothing was found.

Calls from well-meaning persons flooded the switchboard at the New Canaan Police Department. Chief Keller requested that no one telephone unless they had pertinent information. If people wanted to help in the search, he asked that they search in their own area of New Canaan. The New Canaan Women's Club started a telephone campaign to urge townspeople to conduct their own private searches of wooded areas on their property.

Individuals phoned in more stories of mysterious white cars seen near the park and Ralph Scott conducted more interviews, including one of a resident who had a previous arrest for indecent exposure.

Joseph Mount received word of another telephone call made on Friday night to St. Philip's Church in Norwalk that indicated Mary was safe. A reporter from the *Hartford Courant* contacted the FBI, stating that she had received a call from an unidentified male who instructed her to notify Mary's family to put $50,000 in a wastepaper basket in the bathroom of Pippie's restaurant in Hartford, at 8:00 p.m. He stated he would pick up the money at 10:00 p.m. A while later he phoned again and asked the reporter if she had given the message to the family. Ralph Scott relayed the information to the Hartford police and the New Haven office of the FBI.

Later that day, at around 5:00 p.m., Joseph Mount received a phone call from a girl who said she had seen a young white girl in a white vehicle a few days earlier in Paterson, New Jersey. She told Joseph her name was Mary Graham, gave him her phone number, and said she'd call him back when she got more information from her brother. She never called back. To make matters worse, Detective Ralph Scott determined that there was no such number listed in Paterson, New Jersey.

While many people that Memorial Day enjoyed barbecues, family get-togethers and picnics, the Mounts suffered through a series of crank calls and the increasing uncertainty of what happened to Mary. Joseph Mount commented to the press, "We are prepared to do anything in our power to assure Mary's safe return."

Later that evening, The FBI and the Hartford Police placed a dummy package in Pippie's restaurant's wastebasket and staked out the area. At 11:30 p.m., the stakeout was called off because no one attempted to collect the package.

On the morning of Sunday, June 1, the attendees of the Norwalk Community College baccalaureate breakfast observed a moment of silence. A sign outside the Congregational Church near the center of New Canaan read, "Pray For Mary Mount."

Later in the day, two New Canaan police officers headed a search of over 400 volunteers, most of them New Canaan residents. This massive search party covered 370 acres of wooded area in Waveny Park, which is located about a half mile from Kiwanis Park, in an attempt to find a clue about Mary's disappearance. In addition to the police officers and citizens, the group also consisted of firemen, employees of IBM, Boy Scouts and a large group from Norwalk Community College where Joseph Mount taught. Mary's teachers, friends and schoolmates also enlisted in the search. Townsmen equipped with walking sticks combed the hilly terrain. The American Red Cross provided a food canteen. One policeman commented, "You hate to stop looking. Its kind of hard to know when to call it quits."

While the townspeople searched Waveny Park, New Canaan firemen completely pumped out a ten-foot-deep pond located behind the Mount house until only five feet remained in the excavation pit. Just prior to nightfall, they dragged the bottom. The operation was carried out twice, but the search proved futile; Mary was not in the water.

Meanwhile Ralph Scott spoke with a woman who had been at Kiwanis Park until about 6:05 p.m. on Tuesday, the day of Mary's disappearance. She hadn't noticed any men at the park, or any strange vehicles. This indicated that the killer might have arrived at the park after the two Cogswell women left but before Billy left Mary alone. Sadly, Mary had been alone at the park for only 12-15 minutes. In this time frame the abductor had entered the park, saw Mary alone and acted. He had probably just missed Mr. Cogswell coming into the park, or might have even passed him on the road.

Mrs. Beloved, the woman who had phoned on Friday, May 30, phoned again to say that she had once again seen the car she had seen at Kiwanis Park around 4:30 on the day of Mary's disappearance. This time, she had taken down the license plate number. Other calls began to come in about a man who would drive to areas where children were located and watch them. Each witness pointed out to police that the right rear window of the car had a moon-eyes sticker that looked downward. This detail matched Mrs. Beloved's description of the car. Police checks on the vehicle came back to a Louis Jagendorf. The New Canaan police now had their first viable suspect in the Mount case.

At the day's end, with the emergence of Louis Jagendorf as a suspect, the Mounts received a collect call from a man who identified himself as Mr. Foster. The caller said, "Do you recognize my voice? There need be no further searching. I judge from the newspaper you are not taking my call seriously."

Joseph said, "Give me some evidence about Mary, like a shoe or a piece of clothing."

The caller said that would take a lot of time and added, "This is not a deal, it is a business transaction." At this time, a friend of Joseph's picked up the other extension and the caller said, "You can trace this call, but it won't do no good." Joseph got the operator on the line and the call was traced to a phone booth at the Port Authority in New York City. Detective Scott telephoned the FBI office in New York City and though the Port Authority building was checked, the unidentified caller was not apprehended.

The following day, Joseph Mount received another call from a man who said to him, "If you want to see your daughter alive, you will do the following. You will put together $50,000 and throw it on the ground in Times Square in front of the Ostrand Building. I know you will trace this call. If you don't follow this through, your daughter won't be returned alive." This call was traced to the 8th Avenue side of the Port Authority Bus Terminal, street level, opposite the Fannie Farmer Candy Shop. Joseph, torn between hope and fear, broke under the emotional torture and the FBI agents tried their best to calm him in these moments of hysteria.

Looking for even the slightest lead, Ralph Scott questioned even more neighbors and children Mary's age who lived near by or were in the park that day. More girls came to the New Canaan police to report incidences of a man who had tried to pick them up. These girls identified Louis Jagendorf. Later that evening, at about 8 o'clock, another woman phoned Detective Scott and stated that her daughter had been approached by a man who asked her if she wanted a ride. The girl came to headquarters and also identified the man as Jagendorf.

Louis Jagendorf was considered strange and weird-looking. He had thick-rimmed glasses, a crew cut and he tilted his head to the side as he walked. Lieutenant Scott and two FBI agents went to the Jagendorf home. Louis Jagendorf's father stated that on the night of Mary Mount's abduction his son had been at home since four o'clock. While he was speaking Louis pulled into the driveway and his drunken stepmother walked into the room. She kept interfering with the police's interview. Ralph Scott went outside and interviewed Louis in an unmarked police car in the driveway.

Jagendorf's answers were unclear, and police soon discovered he was mentally retarded. He stated that he had been to

New Canaan and he remembered seeing Mrs. Beloved with her two girls but he said that he never tried to pick up girls in or around New Canaan. He remembered hearing about Mary Mount's disappearance from a guy at work who was reading about it in the papers. He said he never drove a white car. The FBI agent advised him that he could contact an attorney at any time. Meanwhile, police took several hair, sand, dirt, and fingerprint samples from Jagendorf's vehicle, which he had just turned in to a used car lot. Jagendorf's attorney would meet with the police the next morning.

By Tuesday, June 3, one week after Mary's disappearance, police still had no clues, though calls and letters continued coming in to police headquarters. Some were exaggerated and others offered advice. The police department did not discount one call. Other citizens phoned tips to the local papers; all information was forwarded to the police.

The police worked on many theories as to the cause of Mary's disappearance. One theory reasoned that an enemy of Mary's father, possibly a student at Norwalk Community College, had snatched Mary. Another less-credible theory reasoned that a woman with a strong maternal instinct kidnapped Mary. The most popular theory, with the best leads, was that a white man driving a white car had abducted her.

Late that Tuesday, a group of nearly 300 persons searched Hoyt's Tree Nursery, a 100-acre tract near the Merritt Parkway, for clues. The group, led by two policemen and two firemen, included students from the New Canaan junior highs and high school, as well as many residents. The state police also rushed to the New Canaan police headquarters late in the day with a computer readout of all white cars registered in the state. The police, along with the FBI, had already checked out 1,000 white cars. The names of 1.7 million motor vehicles registered in Connecticut and 6.1 million registered in New York State were going into the police's computers.

At 6:50 p.m., Louis Jagendorf, his father, and his attorney went to police headquarters. His father stated that Louis had been home since 4:30 p.m. the night of Mary's disappearance. After stating this police informed Louis that someone had seen him at Kiwanis Park at 4:30, Louis admitted to being there and then to driving uptown to East Hills Road (this had been confirmed by another witness). He stated that he drove past the entrance of Kiwanis Park once again at 5:30 on his way home and he saw a woman leaving the park in a station wagon with two children. He ate supper in his room, which was his usual practice at home and he watched "Truth or Consequences," which was on channel five at 7:00 p.m. He stayed home for the rest of the evening. Jagendorf stated again that he never attempted to pick up any girls in New Canaan and that he never asked any girl if she wanted a ride. Detectives advised him that at least three girls reported that he attempted to pick them up.

Louis repeatedly denied the accusations made by the girls. Police asked him if he ever had any girl in his car and he said yes, but they were all over the age of twelve. He insisted that he had not attempted to pick up any girls since he was last warned by the Darien police in May 1968. The Darien police advised him that his operator's license would be taken away if he bothered any girls in the future. Louis stated that he didn't know anything about the missing girl, nor had he seen her at the park. Mrs. Beloved, the woman who had been at Kiwanis Park with her two children, came to headquarters and positively identified Louis Jagendorf as the man she had seen at Kiwanis Park that day.

That day, Joseph Mount received another call from an unidentified male who stated, "I have your daughter in an apartment. Get the FBI out of the house. I want $1,000 for your daughter to be released, will call back." The caller then hung up.

A third massive search was started on Wednesday, June 4, this time by over 200 Boy Scouts who representing four troops in New Canaan. They searched for Mary in a 22-acre Boy Scout camp area on Valley Road in New Canaan. During this search Lieutenant Ralph Scott directed Detective Gene Ready and an FBI agent to conduct a check in the neighborhood of Jagendorf's home. It was now certain that he had approached four girls for rides. They checked 11 homes in Jagendorf's area, and no one could really remember if they had seen him or his father on Tuesday. May 27th.

At 4:00 p.m., Lily Mount received a call from an unidentified male who said, "Tell Mr. Mount I have the kid," and then hung up.

The following day the number of white cars that had been checked by police jumped to 4,000. Mrs. Jagendorf, Louis' stepmother, came to police headquarters first thing in the morning to say that when she had arrived home from work around 6:00 p.m. on Tuesday, May 27, Louis and her husband were already home. Dinner had been at 7:30, with Louis eating in his own room, as was his habit. She stated that he cut the lawn with his father on Wednesday, the day after Mary's disappearance, and that he and his girlfriend were at the Jagendorf home on Thursday. When Detective Ready asked Mrs. Jagendorf if Louis was capable of committing an act of violence, she said "no," but also stated that he had struck her several times.

Along with the detectives, Chief Keller worked 17-hour days trying to find Mary. He stated that New Canaan would no longer conduct any more massive search parties as these had covered all of the larger areas of town. A small task force of policemen still searched and the police expressed their hope that the citizens living in wooded areas would continue to check their areas for any signs of Mary.

On that day, the ninth day since Mary's disappearance, friends of the Mount family offered a $15,000 reward for information leading to her whereabouts. The group who put up the reward established themselves as the sole judges of the person or persons who would be entitled to it.

Several friends of the Mount family, as well as several of Mary's teachers, went and sat with the Mounts at night in an effort to help them cope with their despair. The Mounts recounted the story of how they had visited a psychic in Greenwich to help them to know what happened to Mary. The psychic told them that he saw a man sitting by Mary's side while she played at the sandpile and that this man killed her. The psychic also mentioned something about Wilton, Connecticut.

Fifteen days after the disappearance, neither Chief Keller nor the Mounts had had any sleep. Chief Keller drove the streets of the town in pre-dawn darkness with his walkie-talkie in hand, looking for anything he might have previously overlooked. As Chief Keller drove by the Mount home, he discovered it well-lit at 4 a.m. The anguished family never gave up their vigil by the phone.

For the small, affluent New England town that had never known the horrors of violent crime, the disappearance of Mary Mount was a real tragedy. During the day neighbors of the Mounts brought them baked goods and casseroles. All of the organizations Joseph Mount worked with did all that they could for the family. Students and faculty from Norwalk Community College, where he taught part-time, took part in the Norwalk/New Canaan search. Townspeople and friends helped by offering reward money. All the Mount family wanted was to have Mary back.

Since Joseph was IBM's Scientific Center Manager, the corporation offered its services to the case by sending five computers to New Canaan, along with eight of its top computer experts. They set up three machines in the police department and two at the Mount home. IBM's experts joined forces with the New Canaan police to feed the computers three million names of registered motor vehicles in the state of Connecticut, plus 19 million from New York. They broke down the list of car owners based on whether they had worked in the New Canaan area, whether they had owned or sold a white car, and whether they had a police record. All persons arrested for an offense involving a minor in

Connecticut and in New York were checked out. The computer supplied the police with a town-by-town breakdown of the owners of white cars. Unfortunately, many of the motor vehicle records were not up to date and some individuals were annoyed at being sought for questioning for cars they no longer owned.

Another man called to say that he had ridden his motorcycle into the park at 7:15 on May 27, and he was there until 8:00. While there he noticed a local store's van in the parking lot and young boys playing ball who eventually stopped to go over to the beach area. For all of the activity in Kiwanis Park on May 27, 1969, from 6:24 until 6:40 there were only two individuals in the park during that short time span – Mary Mount and her abductor.

On Saturday, June 7, the adjacent town of Norwalk conducted a search. Headed by Norwalk's deputy police chief, the search party covered 65 acres of open field near the New Canaan town line. Included in the search were Norwalk police department auxiliary and special police handling the group. About 100 students and faculty from Norwalk Community College joined in. These individuals offered to help in the searches in New Canaan but Chief Keller told them to they should try somewhere around the New Canaan/Norwalk town line. On June 8th the reward for any information leading to the whereabouts of Mary Mount rose to $25,000.

Over the next week, the New Canaan police detectives and sergeants conducted interviews with sex offenders, particularly those who had white vehicles. They also interviewed contractors and their employees who worked in the area of the Mount's home. More calls came in from people who had seen white cars in the area at the time of Mary's abduction, and yet another witness stated that he had seen Louis Jagendorf's car at Kiwanis parked between 5:45 and 5:50 p.m. One of the first girls who told the detectives about a man who tried to pick her up, came down to the station and positively identified a photo of Jagendorf. Ralph Scott wanted

Jagendorf to take a lie detector test but his attorney demanded that a psychiatrist examine him before he consented to a polygraph. Although Jagendorf was the leading suspect, not all were convinced he had abducted Mary.

Each day Chief Keller visited the Mounts and brought them their mail, which had been delivered directly to the police station so that police could go through it in search of a possible ransom note. With each visit Chief Keller directly encountered the Mount family's despair and he grew more desperate to find Mary's abductor.

Eighteen days after Mary's disappearance, many still held out hope. The neighboring town of Wilton conducted a final search. Over 85 volunteers searched the Wilton reservoir property, which covered two square miles. Included in the search party were the Chief of the Wilton police, other members of the police department, volunteer firemen, Boy Scouts and many private citizens. The local paper announced the search and invited anyone over 14 years of age to join the search party. Searchers were organized into groups and assigned to a specific working area. The New Canaan Police, FBI, and State Police continued to check white cars in the area, and the IBM executives worked at their computers day and night. The reward price increased by another $1,000.

Since Mary's disappearance, six massive search parties involving more than 1,200 volunteers had combed some 1,771 acres of open space in New Canaan, Wilton, and Norwalk in an attempt to find her. The combined efforts of all of the involved law enforcement agencies and concerned citizens made Mary Mount the most searched-for child in the history of the state of Connecticut and possibly the nation.

CHAPTER THREE

A SAD DISCOVERY

Police dealt with their fair share of crackpots during their search for Mary. In any publicized crime case, these individuals emerge, and sometimes in rather large numbers. One renowned psychic who practiced divination came to Lieutenant Ralph Scott's office with a chain and a map. He pointed the chain at a small cemetery in New Canaan, and said Mary's body could be found there. Police checked the location and found nothing.

Police also checked out a strange local man who drove a bicycle with all sorts of items attached to it. He was known as Bicycle Bob. After police interviewed him, Ralph Scott began getting phone calls from him. Whenever Lieutenant Scott asked Bicycle Bob to identify himself on the phone, he always replied, "007 here," and would go on to report the license plate numbers of all the white cars he had seen that day. It hadn't taken much for Bicycle Bob to begin thinking that he worked for the police. After this incident, he came to be known locally as "007."

Another weird occurrence involved an articulate, conservative-looking man in a three-piece suit. He walked into police headquarters, claiming to have pertinent information about the case. His polished, aristocratic looks told police that he was educated and serious and could, in fact, possess some vital information. When Ralph Scott, New Canaan police Sergeant

Angelostro, and several of the FBI agents questioned the man, he told them, "A few days ago I died and when I died I met Mary and she told me where she was."

Sergeant Angelostro had to hold back his own hysterical laughter and Lieutenant Scott went into a moment of shock and disbelief. They let the man speak, thanked him for coming to them and, after he left, everyone in the room laughed and voiced their disbelief.

By Tuesday, June 17th, which was the three-week anniversary of Mary's disappearance, members of the Metropolitan Regional Council's Committee on Crime were brought into the case. Deputy Chief Fredrick P. Tiani attended a meeting in Darien and briefed top law enforcement officials from Connecticut, New York, and New Jersey on the investigation. This tri-state force now joined the force of FBI agents and police officials who had investigated around the clock since May 27th. Inwardly, some had given up hope that Mary would ever be found.

That same day, high school students Alphonse Cotoia and Gary Brown, decided to go fishing at the Wilton Reservoir. Sixteen-year-old Gary had fished at the reservoir since his grade school years. The reservoir consisted of three bodies of water, and a special permit was required in order to fish there. The two lower bodies of water were divided by a crossway, which you could drive over, but the upper section was less accessible. Gary, who didn't have a fishing permit, always fished at the upper body of water because it was easier to remain hidden from authorities.

Gary and Al drove out over Silvermine Road to Belden Hill Road in Wilton, then swung into Old Huckleberry Hill Road to the old dirt accessway that crossed between the two lower sections of the reservoir. For some reason, they decided to fish in the lower body of water that day, instead of their usual spot at the upper, more hidden body of water. The boys parked and began walking a path parallel to the reservoir, close to the road where they had parked.

They stopped along the water's edge and started to fish along the shore of the pond. At one point they split up and Al continued ahead walking along the shoreline, looking for a better fishing area. Gary walked to catch up to Al and they crossed a swamp area. Gary was five to ten feet away from Al when Al said, "Do you smell that?" Gary commented that he didn't smell anything, and Al added, "It smells like a dead animal." Al and Gary both happened to look in the same direction and, to their horror, they saw a child-sized human skeleton dressed in a pink-flowered sleeveless blouse. Amidst the pink clothing were brown leaves. The skeleton rested in a small pine-needled clearing in the dense underbrush along a path dominated by tall pines.

Though Al stood about 20 feet from the scene and Gary stood 25 to 30 feet away, it was clear that the skull exhibited a hole the size of a golf ball to the size of a tennis ball. After a few terrifying seconds they both uttered, "Mary Mount." They ran as fast as they could back to their car, terrified by what they had seen, and fearing for their own lives.

In the car the boys tried to decide which police department they should contact, New Canaan or Wilton, since they had found the body in Wilton. They decided to go to the New Canaan police. Gary and Al arrived at the New Canaan station and cried to the desk office, "We think we found Mary Mount." They then described to police the skeleton in the woods and soon found themselves in a squad car leading the police to the site.

Lieutenant Scott, Chief Keller, Deputy Chief Tiani accompanied the boys back to the reservoir, as did an FBI agent, three more local officers, and a doctor. The Wilton police were notified. When the boys entered the section of woods that led to Mary's body they pointed the police in the right direction and stood back, unwilling to look at the body again. Later both boys would decide to put this episode behind them and never again talk about it.

When the police arrived, they found the body near a large rock, 48 feet from the water's edge. The body was on its side with arms together and legs drawn up against the stomach, slightly toward the chest with one leg crossed over the other. The ground area around the body appeared to have been cleared away. Mary's legs and head faced towards the woods and her back was against the water. The side of her skull that lay exposed bore a large hole. She was lying face down.

The Wilton police arrived and began working with the New Canaan police to rope off and search the area, take pictures, and make sketches. The Wilton Police conducted a murder investigation because Mary's body was found in Wilton's jurisdiction. Wilton police took several samples of plant life and ground-cover, which appeared to carry splatters of a dark red substance, possibly blood. Officers from the Wilton Police department drove throughout Thursday night to deliver these materials to the FBI lab in Washington D.C. by Friday morning. The materials were entered at the world-renowned criminal lab under a FBI case number that had been assigned on May 27, when Mary disappeared from Kiwanis Park.

Dr. Robert W. Nespor, the Westport-Wilton medical examiner, supervised the removal of the body from the scene to the morgue at the Norwalk Hospital. Dr. Nespor estimated the time of death at three weeks prior, judging from the remains of the skeletal structure, which bore the effects of carnivorous animals.

Police cordoned off the area and posted an all-night guard. They removed the body at 8:30 p.m. and searched the area around the location for clues until darkness halted them at 9 p.m. Authorities returned the next morning and conducted a thorough search to determine if death occurred at the scene. Divers searched the reservoir in search of murder weapons. Ironically, one of the many search parties had searched the southern portion of the reservoir on the previous Sunday until rain halted the effort. One of the volunteers commented, "We didn't go far enough."

Upon discovering Mary's body, the New Canaan Police conducted a vacuum search of Louis Jagendorf's vehicle. The evidence was turned over the Wilton Police and taken to the FBI lab.

At 7:00 p.m. on Tuesday, June 17, Chief Keller arrived at the Mount home to notify Joseph Mount of the discovery of the body. Joseph sadly stated, "I expected it." He went to the Norwalk Hospital, viewed the clothing and said, "Those are my Mary's."

The next morning, reporters were at the Mount home looking for a statement. Joseph Mount opened the door and stepped outside. He looked at the reporters intently with red, slightly swollen eyes, his hands hooked into the rear of his belt. "Yes, I have something to say," he said soberly. "I've been thinking about it all night. But you know I just can't say anything yet."

Joseph gazed absent-mindedly toward the Kiwanis Park. "I've thought a lot during the night, I've even written some thoughts on paper, there are many I want to thank for their efforts. But you see, I just have to wait for positive identification. When that is concluded, I want to say something. Please come back."

On Wednesday morning, New Canaan Police Chief Keller told reporters, "We know now that we have a dangerous criminal in the area. We also know more than we knew before. We knew before that there was a white car. Now we know the direction the car went. It means a lot to us." Chief Keller again appealed for public assistance. "What may seem insignificant to the casual observer may assume tremendous importance when we correlate it with other information we have on hand. We continue to receive telephone calls and letters telling us of drivers of white cars who have suddenly moved or somehow changed their normal habits or are otherwise acting in a way that rouses the caller's suspicions. We have investigated and continue to investigate every one of these leads." Chief Keller urged that anyone who may have observed anything in Kiwanis Park or the reservoir areas around the time of Mary's disappearance or seen anything suspicious involving a white car since the disappearance, to contact the New Canaan Police Department.

Chief Keller looked forward to the possibility of getting more State police aid and FBI support. The discovery of the body in Wilton precluded the continued jurisdiction of the FBI, since they had been involved only on the assumption that Mary had been taken across the state line or that ransom notes might follow the abduction. With the discovery of Mary's body, the FBI continued to assist in the investigation, but not to the extent that they were previously involved. At one point after the abduction, a dozen FBI men worked on the case, but that number now dwindled to half a dozen.

Due to this reduction in manpower, Norwalk's police chief offered additional support from his detective staff and the Lieutenant of the State Police at Troop G in Westport offered a couple of men to the Wilton police department. New Canaan Chief Keller and Wilton Chief Robert J. Northcott were grateful for this help, which bolstered their comparatively small departments. IBM personnel assured Chief Keller of their continuing help in manning several computers on their own time. Other towns and cities near and far also pitched in. At one point, the Westport police chief visited and stated, " I have told my men to consider this case as if it happened in our town, Anything Chief Keller wants us to do, we'll do it." The list of calls from police chiefs throughout the state was endless. The Mary Mount case had more assistance and personnel working on it than any other case in the history of the state.

The support didn't end there. The townspeople did all they could. Some people even offered Chief Keller vacation time at their summer homes in Vermont and New York state. Others invited him to supper at their homes. Chief Keller had kind words about the residents and kind words for Joseph Mount. Keller came to know Joseph, a practicing Baptist, as a very religious man, and admired Joseph greatly for his strength during such a tragic time in his life. "Dr. Mount is a remarkable man," Chief Keller said. "He has been very cooperative with my department and would always confer with me before he did something. It was like he worked for me." Keller also cited the outstanding work being done by his men: "They are all great."

Wednesday, the day after the discovery of the body, the phone at New Canaan Police Headquarters started ringing at 6:30 for desk-men Lloyd C. Cook and James G. Dubay. By 3:00 p.m., both men were exhausted. Though some routine calls came in, the bulk of them concerned the Mary Mount case. Normally, one officer handled the desk. However, that day two men worked it. Between calls, the officers had to cope with the many reporters who swarmed over the department asking to see the chief.

At one point during the afternoon, an elderly woman, a clairvoyant who had traveled from New York City to New Canaan, confided that she, together with the spirits, had predicted the exact location of Mary's body two days before the police found it.
Out in the front of the department, television cameras and men with tape recorders waited to catch someone important involved in the case. Any facts about the case came from Chief Keller, who had undergone terrible strain during the three weeks before Mary's body was found. He kept the news media well informed along with his desk-men, who passed information on to callers.

Ralph Scott instructed Gary Brown and Al Cotoia not talk to anyone about finding the body of Mary Mount. And people certainly did want to talk to the boys. Gary received a phone call from a man who claimed to be with the Wilton police department and wanted to know why Gary didn't go to the Wilton police first. He wanted to meet with Gary to talk more with him about the discovery of Mary's body, and Gary said he would get back to him. When Gary phoned the Wilton police department, he was filled with dread to discover that no such man existed. Most likely it was a reporter who stooped to deceit to get Gary's story, which became well-publicized after the *Stamford Advocate* ran photos of Al and Gary on the front page.

In Wilton, police stopped all motorists using Old Huckleberry Road and asked them if they had remembered anything unusual in the last month. The white car was the only clue the police had to work with. Ralph Scott conducted a neighborhood investigation in the area, but it proved futile.

A two-hour autopsy resulted in positive identification of Mary via dental records. A large hole on the side toward the back of the skull indicated a severe fracture. The autopsy revealed that death possibly resulted from this massive skull fracture brought on by at least one blow from a blunt instrument. Dr. Cody stated, "The autopsy performed on Mary Mount disclosed that she suffered a fractured skull. The fracture was extensive and could be the probable cause of death." He believed the skull injury "was the result of a heavy, weighted instrument, possibly a hammer." The doctor estimated the time of death at three weeks, indicating that Mary's abductor had killed her shortly after kidnapping her.

The autopsy and chemical analysis provided no observable evidence of sexual assault. Since Mary's body was found clothed in the same clothing in which she disappeared and her clothing was not in disarray except that her feet were bare, police did not believe she was sexually assaulted.

Wilton Police Chief Northcott announced at 12:45, following completion of the autopsy, that the body had been identified. New Canaan Police Chief Keller expected to find a suspect and he felt that finding Mary's body narrowed the search and provided the police with a direction in which to go. Police commented that there had been no legitimate demand for ransom, and Chief Keller believed the suspect would probably be a sex offender and a person inclined to commit acts of violence. Chiefs Keller and Northcott agreed that the killer must be a person who knows the area well, because of the location in which Mary's body was found. The pathway leading to Mary's body was one that was known by fishermen looking for spots to fish that would also keep them hidden from view of the town workers who would kick them off the property if they were found fishing. "No trespassing" signs mark the grounds, and trespassing hikers, fishermen, and nature lovers are asked to leave when spotted by water company employees.

The location where the boys found Mary's body is about three miles from the New Canaan town line and about six miles from Kiwanis Park. Oddly, it was approximately the same area where two Norwalk teenagers left the body of an 18-year-old boy they murdered for his car in 1964.

Joseph Mount called his family together to tell them that Mary's body had been found in a wooded area in a nearby town. Joseph Jr., David, and Billy had dreaded this event for some time. With the news of Mary's confirmed death, mourning now replaced the boys' hope that somehow their sister might be alive. Meanwhile, in Kiwanis Park, the sand pile where Mary Mount played and disappeared three weeks earlier became the bottom of the manmade pool that hundreds of children now enjoyed. Neighbors brought casseroles and condolences to the Mount home. An exhausted Joseph Mount issued a formal statement on Wednesday, thanking all of those whose help and prayers supported his family during a period of anxiety:

"We have just received word that our precious daughter, Mary, is dead. We are exceedingly grateful for the love that has been abundantly showered on our family during this difficult period of anxious uncertainty. The faith, hope, love, support, and especially the prayers of our friends, neighbors and, in some cases, sympathetic strangers, has comforted and sustained us greatly. Today we accept the Lord's will in the case of Mary's life on Earth. The Lord gave and the Lord hath taken away. Blessed be the name of the Lord."

Friends of the Mount family immediately initiated a memorial scholarship at Norwalk Community College, where Dr. Mount taught classes. The scholarship, known as the Mary Mount Memorial Scholarship Fund, is used to help disadvantaged children gain a college education. The group who founded the scholarship chose to remain anonymous and suggested that all friends of the Mounts as well as those harboring sympathy for the family could best honor Mary's memory by sending contributions to the college in her name.

The Stamford Chamber of Commerce called on employers in the area to report who did not come to work May 28th, the day after Mary disappeared. Experts fed this information into computers to help find the alleged killer. Scores of persons came to Wilton police headquarters during the day to volunteer information they believed might help the investigation. Chief Northcott of Wilton said every bit of information either brought into or phoned to headquarters would be treated as if "it were the biggest thing in the world."

Despite the cooperation of both police departments and the unified response by their Chiefs, the Wilton Police Department soon after discontinued working with the New Canaan Police on the homicide. Wilton detectives found Mary Mount's second shoe in the woods on the path the killer carried her body and never informed the New Canaan Police until years later. The location of the shoe revealed a different path that Mary's killer took from the one that the New Canaan Police speculated.

On Thursday, June 19, 1969, a private funeral service and burial for Mary was held at New Canaan Methodist Church. The short service was witnessed by the Mount family and about a dozen friends and relatives. All of the teachers from Mary's grade school attended, along with the principal. Lieutenant Ralph Scott and one of the FBI agents also attended the funeral. The group listened to the words of Reverend Davis with solemnity; many wept quietly.

Later, family and friends accompanied Mary's body to a plot at New Canaan's Lakeview Cemetery, where they held a brief committal service. Six bouquets and two large flower arrangements stood at the head of Mary's white casket. An overturned cardboard vase with the name "Mary" scrawled on the bottom with a green marker stood against the bows and flowers.

One of the school's counselors urged Mary's teacher to continue to visit the Mounts. Sometime after the funeral, she visited the Mount house. Lily Mount, now an obviously broken and saddened woman, showed Mary's teacher the clothes that still hung in Mary's closet and the room which remained exactly as Mary had last left it.

Mary's teacher asked Lily to come to school and help with an art project. The teacher wanted to build a giant whale with an opening in its belly where children could sit and read, but she didn't know how to go about it. Lily gladly obliged. She went to the school and determined that the inner structure of the whale should be made out of chicken wire and they would build from there. Lily also taught the other volunteering mothers how to go about making this large item. The children enjoyed Lily Mount's visits to their classroom, and she enjoyed being there as well. Going to Mary's school provided some comfort but nothing ever really healed the gaping hole in Lily Mount's heart.

With Mary's death came the end of the Mounts' hopes and dreams for their daughter. In three weeks' time their world, which held promises of only good things, deteriorated. New Canaan now represented to them the soul-breaking experience from which they would never recover. The home they had built brought them great sadness because of Mary's empty room; the back yard that she no longer played in bore an emptiness that was abysmal. The following winter, when the trees were barren, the Mounts could see to Kiwanis Park and were forced to view the area from which Mary's murderer had abducted her. Within two years the Mounts would leave New Canaan and never return.

With the passing of years, new residents who moved into town brought their children to Kiwanis Park to swim and to play on the swings. Many had no idea of the child who had been played at the sandpile when a killer abducted and murdered her to satisfy a hellish urge.

The Mounts' lives went on. Dr. Mount and his sons achieved all of the things they had hoped for, but without their precious Mary beside them. With her loss came years of mourning and a broken place in their hearts that could never be fixed.

Other children are buried in the cemetery where Mary's grave lies, but all of these children sadly lost their lives to an illness or accident. Many people, upon seeing Mary's grave, would assume the same fate befell this 10-year-old girl.

At the time her body was found, the rewards offered for information concerning Mary Mount amounted to $26,000. However, the reward carried with it a provision that all claims must be filed with the New Canaan police within 48 hours after the discovery of Mary's whereabouts. Gary Brown and Alphonse Cotoia had discovered Mary's body on Tuesday, June 17 and by Friday, June 20, the reward remained uncollected. It expired later that day, at 5:21 p.m.

Neither of the boys had the heart to claim the reward. Although Ralph Scott urged them to claim the money, Gary and Al couldn't in good conscience take the check and use it knowing that the money had been given to them because a young girl had died tragically. Gary felt that if he claimed the money, nothing positive could have emerged from any purchases he made with it. He suggested that it be given to a charity.

A few days later, police received another lead concerning a 28-year-old man driving a white automobile in Port Chester, New York. This man had been arrested for raping a three-and-a-half-year-old girl and leaving her in the woods. On hearing of the arrest, New Canaan detectives rushed to interrogate the man to see if there was a possible connection with the death of Mary Mount. This perpetrator was willing to take a lie detector test in the Mount case, a crime that he described as "horrible." New Canaan police concluded that the chances of this man being Mary Mount's killer were slim, since the white auto he drove didn't match the one witnesses saw driving away from Kiwanis Park on May 27.

    Police continued to receive leads on men who showed an abnormal interest in young girls. Two young men came into headquarters and said they had seen a man in a white car at the reservoir. A drawing was made of the man seen that day and the picture was given to area detectives.

    Louis Jagendorf remained the police's best suspect. His family refused to allow him to take a polygraph. Police did get hair samples from Jagendorf and sent them to the FBI crime lab, along with samples sent from his car. Authorities did not find any evidence that Mary Mount had been in Jagendorf's car but it was discovered that he had lied to police about attempting to pick up young girls. He was later arrested by the Darien police on February 25, 1970 for breach of peace when he picked up two teenage girls in his vehicle and asked them questions about what type of underwear they were wearing. Lieutenant Ralph Scott felt that Jagendorf had a good alibi for the time of Mary's abduction and although he did make a habit of picking up young girls, he never harmed one. In time, new suspects would emerge who the New Canaan police would favor over Jagendorf.

CHAPTER FOUR

RIDERS ON THE STORM

Mary Mount's brutal and senseless murder startled the residents of Fairfield County. The wealth and affluence of the area generally sheltered the locals from these horrors. Their shock would have been even greater had they known that two serial killers were operating in the area at the time of Mary Mount's disappearance. Both became suspects in her murder. A third serial killer would emerge years later. He lived in the most affluent section of New Canaan and would later become a suspect in Mary's death. His crimes were so brutal that investigators dubbed him "Hannibal Lecter come to life."

On May 18, 1969, one week before Mary Mount's abduction, 11-year-old Diane Toney's parents reported her missing. She was last seen at the Freddy Fixer Parade in downtown New Haven. Three days after Mary Mount's abduction, 14-year-old Dawn Cave disappeared on Memorial Day, Friday May 30, 1969 while walking about a mile from her home in Bethany, a small town about 40 miles from New Canaan. Two girls discovered Dawn Cave's body in a hay field on July 1, 1969.

State police immediately tried to determine if there was any link between the murder/abduction of Mary Mount and the death of Dawn Cave. Police cited a number of similarities between the murders of the two girls. Both girls had fractured skulls. Mary Mount was slain by a blow to the head with a blunt instrument and

Dawn Cave was murdered with a rock from a nearby crumbling stone wall. The bludgeon that fractured Mary's skull was never found, although divers searched the bottom of the reservoir. Police believed a maniac was at large and that the killer of the girls may have been the same man, although Chief Keller stated publicly that there was no evidence that the same person had murdered Mary Mount and Dawn Cave.

A Bethany couple reported that they had seen a "light-colored" car parked not far from the remote field where Dawn's body lay in a makeshift grave made of stones. Both bodies were hidden in seldom-used areas near lightly-traveled roads.

Investigators expressed the opinion that all three girls – Dawn Cave, Diane Toney and Mary Mount – were probably killed within hours after they disappeared. The Toney family voiced grievances at the FBI for paying a great deal of attention to the Mary Mount case while ignoring their own daughter. They attributed this to their being of African descent. The FBI suspected foul play by a member of Diane Toney's family and felt that her case differed from that of Mary Mount. Diane's body had not yet been found, but police assumed she was dead.

Police checked also investigated the murder of nine-year-old Wanda Maldonado in Brooklyn, New York, who disappeared while playing near her home on July 3. Her body was found on July 9, in an abandoned railroad car 20 blocks away. Area residents reported seeing a white man in a white car trying to entice young girls into his vehicle.

On July 3, 1969, anonymous contributors identifying themselves as "concerned citizens" offered a reward of $50,000 for information leading to the arrest of the killer of Mary Mount. When the reward expired on August 7, it was extended to September 2, 1969. Only skimpy leads came in to the authorities. Such generous rewards remaining unclaimed revealed some information about the killer. If he was local, he was a loner.

As murder after murder occurred, the New Canaan police continued to speak to many more possible suspects including two suspects held in the Dawn Cave case: Donald Whiting and James Pappas. Donald Whiting's doctor, Dr. Robert Miller, felt that Whiting, a paranoid schizophrenic, might have committed the Mary Mount and Dawn Cave homicides. Whiting agreed to take a polygraph but the hairs in his car did not match Mary Mount's hair.

Diane Toney's body was discovered October 2, 1969, in a heavily wooded area off Route 80 in North Guilford. Diane died of a fractured skull. The FBI lab in Washington, DC identified her remains, but some members of her family refused to believe that the body was Diane's. The remains were never claimed, and they sat in a cardboard box in a closet at the New Haven state's attorney's office until they were turned over to Guilford police. Police raised the money to bury the remains in 1996.

On August 13, 1970, three mentally retarded people were murdered in the West Rock area of New Haven. All were bludgeoned to death with rocks. The first one 20-year-old William White, was killed in West Rock Park. He was found naked with his face smashed in and his clothes thrown about. The two girls – Donna Schlitter, 15, and Sandra Hedler, 23 – were found about six hours later underneath a vent tower a few miles away. Both were face down, and had been raped before they were murdered. All three were killed with rocks; the killer had carried no weapons, but used what was handy at the murder sites. At the time of these murders, police consulted leading psychiatrists who felt that the murders of the three retarded youths and those of Mary Mount, Dawn Cave, and Diane Toney were all linked and committed by the same person. Detective Bill White became the leading detective on the case.

A little over a month later, on September 21, 1970, five-year-old Jennifer Noon disappeared while walking home from school for lunch. Her body was found eight days later on September 29, 1970, in a heavily wooded area near Sleeping Giant

State Park in Hamden. Jennifer died of a fractured skull. Her head had been beaten so savagely that her skull actually split in two pieces. With Jennifer Noon's death, the New Haven police called on all surrounding police departments and inquired if they had unsolved, open cases. Although Lieutenant Ralph Scott was called in to help on the case, New Canaan's department was not in on the investigation.

Police arrested a man named Harold Mead in December 1970, after collecting a good deal of evidence that pointed to him having committed these murders. Many eyewitnesses had seen Mead driving around with the retarded youths and Mead himself boasted about the murders to an acquaintance. When police confronted him with the mounting evidence against him, however, he remained reluctant to confess to the murders. Detectives discovered that in 1968, Mead had been arrested on a charge of attempted kidnapping after walking up to a 16-year-old girl with a starter pistol and attempting to get her into his vehicle. He received two years probation for this charge.

Harold Mead's father owned a gas station on Route 67, not far from where Dawn Cave's body was found. On the day of Jennifer Noon's disappearance, Mead's car was being worked on and he had borrowed one of the cars from his father's gas station, which he could have used to commit the murder.

A milkman who had seen Mead's photo on television after he had been arrested in another case told authorities that Mead was the man he saw with Jennifer Noon the day she was abducted. The coroner found that Jennifer had eaten a doughnut before she died and a witness from a doughnut shop saw Mead buying doughnuts that morning. Detective Bill White also discovered that Mead collected photographs of young children.

In an effort to get a confession out of Mead for the murder of the three retarded youths, Thomas Gordina, Mead's public defender, made a deal with the State Prosecutor Arnold Markle. If

Mead confessed to the murders of the three retarded youths, he wouldn't be questioned about any of the other homicides. Although Bill White considered Mead a strong suspect in the murders of Dawn Cave, Mary Mount, and Jennifer Noon, he felt unsure about Mead's participation in the murder of Diane Toney. Diane was last seen at the Freddy Fixer Parade, an event that was not attended by white people. A white man at that parade would have stood out amid the black participants.

Gordina felt that Mead was guilty of the murders of the three girls, but that prosecutors had enough evidence, including Mead's own confession, to convict him of the murder of the three retarded individuals. That alone would guarantee that Mead would be put away for life.

At the time of Harold Mead's arrest, Lieutenant Ralph Scott was no longer helping with the New Haven cases. Although a New Haven newspaper wrote an article at that time, connecting Mead to the Mary Mount murder, New Haven police, intent on solving their own case, didn't phone the New Canaan police concerning Mead. When Ralph Scott got word about Mead's murders and confession, he attempted to speak with Mead concerning Mary Mount's murder, but Gordina refused to let Scott speak with him. Since there were no witnesses who had seen Mead in New Canaan and because of the absence of physical evidence tying Mead to the scene, there were no grounds for overturning Gordina's denial of Scott's request. A New Haven detective, on behalf of the New Canaan Police Department, asked Mead if he had killed Mary Mount. Mead said that he didn't remember.

In the opinion of Lieutenant Scott and other detectives at the New Canaan Police Department, Harold Mead stood out as the best suspect in the Mount case. The problem was placing him in New Canaan on May 27, 1969, the day of Mary's abduction. Mead held a job as a milkman, and rumor had it he was also a Good Humor man; these positions might have brought him to New Canaan. Mead is also a popular name in New Canaan; one of the town's main parks is called Mead Park. He might have been distantly related to the Meads in New Canaan and this might have brought him there. The area where Mary's body was found was a spot known by fisherman; Mead was an avid outdoorsman who had maps of state parks, owned a boat and fished.

On April 6, 1972, Mead was found guilty of three counts of second degree murder for the three retarded youths. He received a life sentence for each of the three counts. Though Connecticut had the death penalty at that time, Mead did not receive the death penalty for these murders.

State's Attorney Gordina miscalculated when he assumed that the confession for the triple murder would put Mead away for life and put an end to his killing spree. After being incarcerated for 13 years, Harold Mead started to be released on furloughs. In 1985, Mead had 184 one-day furloughs and 68 weekend leaves. He met and married his second wife while on furlough and, on the last weekend of June 1992, the couple celebrated their second anniversary by renting a cabin on the shore. The next day, the body of 43-year-old Linda Raynor was found at Hammonasset Beach State Park, in a remote section frequented mainly by fishermen. Her skull had been crushed with a rock.

Less than two months after the Raynor killing, Mead was removed from the furlough program and placed in the highest security level below death row inmates. He has not been let out of prison since. Although Mead has admitted various pieces of information concerning the murders of Dawn Cave and Diane Toney to his fellow inmates, he has never admitted to any of the murders to the media or anyone in law enforcement. He believes that there is still a chance that he might get out of prison and he doesn't want to do anything that will jeopardize his release. After the publication of a *Hartford Courant* article that linked Mead to the murders of young girls, he received a severe beating in prison and he and his wife have not spoken to anyone about the murders since.

Mead is a serial killer who police arrested early in his career. The efforts of the New Haven Police Department along with Bill White, the chief detective who worked the case, were responsible for apprehending Mead before his body count continued to climb. White would have seen Mead indicted for each of the murders if it wasn't for the deal struck by Thomas Gordina, who now resides as a Superior Court Judge.

Harold Mead wasn't the only serial killer operating in Connecticut at the time of the Mount murder. There was another who dumped the bodies of his victims within a few miles of New Canaan and police would briefly consider this killer as a suspect in the Mary Mount murder.

On May 3, 1968, the body of 22-year-old Donna Robbins of Stamford Connecticut was found. In September 1968, about 200 yards from where Robbins' body was found, police found the body of Gloria Conn, 19, of Mount Vernon, New York. Both women had been strangled with their brassieres.

In April 1969, one month before the disappearance of Mary Mount, the third victim, 31-year-old Rosellen Pazda of Stamford, was found in an area of the Merritt Parkway that was located only a few miles from the New Canaan town line. Her body was so badly decomposed that medical authorities were unable to determine the cause of death. An autopsy established that the probable cause was strangulation.

Police discovered that the three women knew each other and they questioned common acquaintances in hopes of turning up a suspect. All of the victims were black women and all had been strangled. The fourth body, that of Gail Thompson, 17, of Stamford, was discovered about a mile from where the other three were found.

Many African-Americans felt that nothing was being done to solve the case because the victims were black and had questionable backgrounds; they were prostitutes. Citizens formed an ad hoc committee and wrote outraged letters to Stamford Police

Chief Kinsella, though authorities maintained investigations had been conducted at a strenuous pace from the time the first body was discovered in May 1968.

On March 17, 1972, police booked a 42-year-old postal worker by the name of Benjamin Miller for the Parkway killings. Miller, married and with one son, had worked as a dispatcher for the Darien post office for the previous 10 years. Miller, an active suspect for six months, had undergone psychiatric treatment at a mental hospital in 1951 and was committed again a month before his arrest.

Miller's co-workers were shocked at discovering that he was a suspect in the "bra murders." They described him as a loner who talked mostly about religion. Miller gave street-corner sermons in the area of Stamford where the women were believed to have been abducted. The neighborhood has heavy pedestrian traffic as late as 3:00 a.m. Miller's neighbors referred to him as "the preacher."

When police apprehended Miller, they checked out the possibility that he might have murdered Mary Mount and reopened her case. Lieutenant Ralph Scott discovered that Ben Miller rented an apartment in New Canaan on Main Street. The Bra Murders bore no similarities to the Mount murder but, with the Mount case reopened, Lieutenant Scott decided to pursue Mead, who agreed to talk to detectives about anything they wanted to discuss, provided he was transferred from prison to a state hospital. His wife would act as his spokesperson. Mead's attorney contacted the state's attorney but he refused Mead's proposal. Thus Mead was never questioned in the Mount case, despite Scott's efforts.

Chief Kinsella described the search for the Bra Murderer as "the longest and most arduous" in the history of the Stamford police. However, in spite of their apparent success in capturing the person responsible for those murders, evidence began to surface that suggested another individual might have committed these killings and that Miller might have been framed by a police department that needed a conviction. According to Bruce Shapiro, whose article, "Framed," appeared in the 1991 issue of *Connecticut* magazine, after Miller's arrest, a state trooper came upon a man at the Merritt Parkway's Den Road exit, in the act of strangling an unclothed, unconscious black woman. Police arrested him and discovered facts that cast doubts on the Miller arrest. The new suspect, Robert Lupinacci, had been arrested and prosecuted for rape in 1966. The victim dropped the charge because she was too frightened to testify. Lupinacci cruised downtown Stamford the night Gloria Conn disappeared, and other prostitutes had long suspected him of the murders. According to Bruce Shapiro:

"Gail Thompson was last seen alive in a car whose description matched Lupinacci's, and one witness recalled seeing his car parked near the Parkway the day that Thompson was killed. Most startlingly, near Gail Thompson's body police had recovered a pornographic playing card – a queen of hearts. When Lupinacci was arrested, a deck of similar pornographic playing cars was found in his car trunk – minus the queen of hearts."

Interviews with Lupinacci's neighbors and co-workers revealed a "vicious, mean man" who beat his children severely and harassed a neighbor with obscene phone calls. Lupinacci was also an unabashed racist.

When Stamford detectives were in pursuit of Ben Miller, Lupinacci one day approached Stamford police officer Paul Romanos, whom he knew casually, and asked about the Bra Murders investigation, wanting to know when the area around the crime scenes would be staked out, exactly where the stakeouts were, and how long the stakeouts would continue. In the course of the same conversation, Lupinacci told a startled Romanos that not all the dead women had been strangled with their bras. Romanos reported Lupinacci to his colleagues in the police department as a possible suspect, but Stamford detectives never pursued the lead.

When the state police sent Lupinacci's file to State's Attorney Gormley's office, Gormley ignored the file because he felt he had the confessions to the murders so there was no need to investigate another suspect. In the late 1980s, a defense attorney hired by Benjamin Miller got the court to see that the information Gormley had withheld had been "sufficient to undermine confidence" in the fair outcome of Miller's trial. Miller went back to court and the judge dismissed the case, releasing him after 18 years of serving time for murders he claimed he did not commit.

The murders did stop after Miller was apprehended for the crimes and after Lupinacci's arrest. Either Miller was indeed the killer or Lupinacci knew that if he killed again while Miller was put away, all suspicion would point to him.

In the late 1960s, when the abduction and murder of Mary Mount occurred, affluent Fairfield County residents felt safe, despite the fact that only a few miles from the place of Mary's abduction, another murderer was killing women. If this wasn't shocking enough, more than 30 years after the Mount murder, New Canaan police reopened the case to examine the possibility that yet another serial killer was responsible for her murder.

Thirty-one years after Mary Mount's body was found, New Canaan police reopened the investigation when serial killer Hadden Clark, who was serving time in a Maryland prison, confessed to prison officials that he committed more murders than those for which he was incarcerated. New Canaan police discovered that Hadden had once lived in New Canaan's posh West School District and for a time he had attended West School. Although many people considered all of New Canaan affluent, realtors marketed West School as the superior school because New Canaan's most expensive homes were located in that area. In 1999, when the town made plans to send some of New Canaan's children to South School, another elementary school in town, because of overcrowding at West School, residents hired attorneys and threatened law suits over the thought of their children having to mingle with the children of South School.

While most serial killers come from middle- to low-income families, Hadden Clark's father held a doctorate in chemistry, made a comfortable living as an industrial executive, and provided his family with a succession of homes in wealthy and affluent communities. Mr. Clark suffered from manic depression, often slapped his wife around in front of the children, and jumped from one company to another, seeking a level of affluence he couldn't attain. Both of Hadden Clark's parents were active alcoholics. Bradfield, the Clarks' eldest son, is serving 18 years to life in prison for murdering a co-worker in 1984 and dismembering her body in his apartment. It was his first and last offense. The Clarks' eldest son, Geoff, a biologist for the Food and Drug Administration, is a manic depressive who controls his illness with medication.

Hadden's problems added to the dysfunction within the Clark family because he became a major family concern. Experts have found that many serial killers suffered head injuries when they were young children, and Hadden had many of these. His problems began at birth with, oxygen deprivation and frontal lobe dysfunction; he also suffered a head injury at birth when a doctor forcefully used forceps to deliver him. Hadden had difficulties walking which caused him to fall constantly, striking his head. Despite expensive therapy, Hadden continued to fall often.

At school, Hadden Clark was a loner, unable to relate to other kids and often teased. After high school in 1972, he enrolled in the Culinary Institute of America in Hyde Park, New York, and graduated two years later. Hadden quit or was fired from more than a half a dozen kitchen jobs. At one job, co-workers noted his propensity for drinking blood from drained beef. Hadden tended to overreact to criticism and decided that people were out to get him. He was a skilled chess player, artist, and cook, but he was unable to connect with people.

In 1982, Hadden entered the Navy and worked as a cook, but he was discharged in 1985 after exhibiting bizarre behavior. The psychiatrist concluded that he suffered from paranoid schizophrenia manifested by persecutory and grandiose delusions.

After being discharged, Hadden went to live with his brother Geoff in Silver Springs, Maryland. Hadden's behavior unnerved Geoff and scared his fiancé, Stephanie; they asked Hadden to leave. Hadden moved out, but he returned to Geoff's house on May 31, 1986, to pick up the remainder of his belongings. While Hadden was alone in the house that day, six-year-old Michele Dorr, whose father lived two doors down, came to the Clark home to look for Geoff's niece, who was her favorite playmate. Hadden slashed Michele with a butcher knife and drove her remains to a remote location to place her body in a makeshift grave. At 5:30, Carl Dorr showed up at Geoff's to ask if anyone had seen Michele. When police cars started arriving and word of Michele's disappearance got around, Geoff was among the first to mention Hadden's name to detectives.

Sadly, detectives immediately suspected Carl Dorr. A polygraph taken by Dorr erroneously revealed that he might have known who killed his daughter. The police considered him their best suspect and aggressively sought to gather enough evidence to arrest him. They felt he had a violent enough temper to have killed Michele, had ample opportunity, and a motive both emotional– revenge against his wife – and financial. Three weeks before Michele vanished, Dorr's child support payments had increased from $250 per month to $400.

A gardener who worked in the neighborhood told police that on the afternoon of May 31, a man had let him into Geoff Clark's house to use the phone. The gardener said he'd seen a small girl with the man and she matched Michele's description. Detectives got hold of Clark's military record and learned that he'd been discharged from the Navy for psychiatric reasons. When

Detectives questioned Hadden, he denied having seen Michele at Geoff's house on May 31. Detectives checked his time card and learned that he had punched into work at 2:46 p.m. on that day, and he had arrived at work with a bandage on one of his hands. When questioned at length on June 8, Hadden cried, vomited, and said that he may have blacked out and done something he couldn't remember. Police terminated the interview when Clark called his psychologist and attorney.

To count Hadden Clark as a suspect, police needed to know the time Michele Dorr was last seen. Carl Dorr figured he had last seen her at about 2:10 p.m. Police didn't believe Hadden could have abducted and murdered the girl, drove to Wheaton, biked to work and punched in at 2:46 p.m. Carl later stated that he settled for 2:10, that it "sounded like it could be right." He had been through a lot, and later realized that Michele had probably gone out between 12:15 and 2:00 p.m. But, his statement of 2:10 went into the case file. Meanwhile, detectives learned that the Dorr's divorce had not been civil and Mrs. Dorr signed an affidavit stating that her husband Carl had threatened to "meet our daughter, age six, at the bus stop to abduct her." This statement fueled suspicions that Carl Dorr was their man.

However, detectives on the Dorr case never gave up on investigating Hadden Clark. Whenever word reached them he had been arrested, they would investigate the circumstances of each arrest, hoping to discover some link to the Michele Dorr case. That link came six years later.

In the early 1990s, Hadden Clark regularly attended church-sponsored lunches for the homeless in Bethesda, Maryland, where he told church volunteers that he was eager to do yard work. Penny Houghteling, a psychiatric social worker, found Hadden odd, but childlike and eager to please. She hired him to do some gardening for her. Penny's daughter Laura was home alone when Hadden showed up one day to do some gardening. Penny had gone out of town.

When Laura Houghteling didn't show up for work the following Monday, she was soon reported missing. Hadden had been fastidious about cleaning's Laura's bedroom of all traces of blood from her stabbing death. However, a pillowcase from Laura's bed was discovered in woods a few hundred yards from the house. A technician turned up a bloody thumbprint belonging to Hadden Clark.

When detectives first questioned Hadden, he offered an alibi, just as he had when he was questioned in 1986 about Michele Dorr. During the interrogation, police tried to discover where Hadden had buried the bodies, and if there was any chance Laura might still be alive. Hadden said nothing. At times he spoke to detectives in a woman's voice, declaring his name was "Hadeen." At other times he babbled like an infant. He finally offered the police a hint that the bodies were buried in New Jersey. Clark went on to be arrested and convicted in the murders of Michele Dorr and Laura Houghteling and was sentenced to two consecutive 30-year sentences.

While in prison at the turn of the millennium, Clark confessed to police that he had killed more victims and offered details of torturing and cannibalizing some of them. One investigator speculated that Clark cooperated with police because it allowed him to relive his crimes. Investigators speculated that Clark could have killed as many as 11 people. He told police his grisly stories, but none of the facts matched what was known about the unsolved cases police were trying to close. It seemed that Hadden Clark had read about other murders and was trying to take credit for them.

In January 2000, the Wellfleet Police Department in Massachusetts brought Hadden Clark to Wellfleet to search his grandfather's property for victims. Clark claimed to have picked up two women in the 1980s, killed them, and buried them at his grandfather's place in Cape Cod. Clark agreed to talk to the police under one condition: that they give him women's clothing to wear. Police provided him with a skirt – which Clark complained was too large for him – a bra, underpants, and stockings. After taking Clark to his grandfather's home, all police found was a bucket of jewelry, including some belonging to Laura Houghteling, whom Clark had killed in 1992.

    Clark was then transported to Connecticut to talk to authorities about murders that had occurred there, one of which was the 1969 murder of Mary Mount. Hadden claimed to have known Mary and hinted at having committed her murder. It became apparent to many officers that Hadden was "a piece of work" and "a real nut." He couldn't provide bodies, and his stories didn't match the facts. Hadden was trying to make a name for himself. Police knew that he had brutally murdered a small child and a young woman. He very well might have committed other murders but not as many as he would have liked everyone to believe.

    Of these four men – Harold Mead, Benjamin Miller, Robert Lupinacci, and Hadden Clark – Harold Mead became the best suspect in the Mount murder, along with another individual who killed during this time. This killer's crimes would be the next to shock New Canaan's residents and be talked about for years to come.

CHAPTER 5

THE RICE MURDERS

On December 10, 1970, John Rice, Sr. sat in his car driving home from work, anticipating that the day would progress as all others. He looked forward to relaxing once he got home. When Rice opened the door to his house, the scene within changed his life forever and shook the spirit of every New Canaan resident.

The Rices moved to New Canaan in 1961 with hopes of establishing a better life for themselves and their children. Janet Rice, a nurse, had grown up in Byram; a small section of Greenwich, Connecticut's wealthiest community. John had been raised in the working-class city of New Rochelle, New York, only minutes away from Greenwich's wealth and beauty.

John and Janet Rice married on July 12, 1950, in New Hampshire in their early twenties. At the time, John Rice finished serving in the Navy. Three years later, Janet gave birth to the their eldest son, John Jr. Five months after John's birth, Janet Rice conceived again and Stephen followed John by only 14 months. Two years later, Janet delivered a daughter, Nancy. When the Rices moved to New Canaan in August 1961, they left New Rochelle, where John Sr. had been earning his living in the restaurant business. Janet had been working as a staff nurse at New Rochelle Hospital, where all three of her children were born. Nancy started kindergarten in New Canaan, Stephen, second grade and John entered third grade.

When the Rices first moved to New Canaan, John Sr. opened the Candlelight Restaurant, a small eatery that served lunch and dinner but did not have a liquor license. He rented space in New Canaan's downtown area from long-time town resident Jerrol Silverberg, a criminal attorney who owned commercial property in New Canaan's shopping district. Though many are said to have liked the restaurant, it wasn't profitable. Rice closed it down after several months and went to work in Stamford as a manager for Food Management Services, where he obtained the position of cook and cafeteria director at Hi-Standard Co. in Hamden, a gun manufacturing company.

Janet continued working as a nurse. Her coworkers found her warm and hardworking. When Nancy entered high school, Janet enrolled at the Stamford branch of the University of Connecticut to take courses in history, zoology, and biology in anticipation of going on to earning a degree. Janet Rice often spoke fondly about her husband. The nurses viewed the Rices as a close-knit family who enjoyed being with one another. The family lived in a newly-painted, 25-year-old, two-story house with a two-car garage and a well-kept yard. A large black eagle insignia adorned the house's facade while a smaller replica rested above the garage door. The yard, heavily populated with maples and fir trees, provided a shady patio in the rear. The Rice's fenced in the backyard to contain their dogs.

The Rice's middle-class neighborhood didn't compare with the wealthier sections of town where New York executives lived. In fact, New Canaan's only low-income housing project was located near the Rice home.

Unlike the Mount family, who represented the typical New Canaan residents, the Rices were considered strange by many who knew them. At age 14, Nancy Rice was considered pleasant, but horribly shy and homely. One of her classmates described her as "a victim of her face," the most unattractive girl in school. Nancy had inherited her father's beady eyes, her mother's long, thin nose, and both parents' pale complexion. Excess pounds sat on her already large, square frame. Her stringy, flat hair was often left unbrushed and greasy. As a reflection of Nancy's pitiful self-image, she wore old-fashioned clothes. For all of this, the kids routinely made fun of her. Rumor had it that Nancy had lice. One girl talked about organizing a group of girls to wash Nancy's hair and redress her.

Redheaded, bespectacled John also suffered ridicule from fellow students because of his severe acne, which continued from his pockmarked face to the back of his neck. His acne was so bad that people described the back of his neck as looking raw. John Jr. was overweight and had an underbite that made his jaw appear disfigured. To make matters worse, John entered puberty earlier than most boys and his classmates picked on him for being big and awkward. His large head and fixed, empty stare made one want to knock and ask if anyone was home. John also dressed behind the times. While many of the students wore longer hair and John Lennon-style glasses, John Rice, Jr. wore thick, horn-rimmed glasses, a crew cut, and khaki pants that were too short, showing his white socks.

Janet Rice made it known at work that her son John stood as the shining star of the family. She frequently boasted about John's scholastic achievements and Boy Scout work. John, as a senior patrol leader, assisted the scoutmasters on trips and camp-outs. Stephen became a member of the troop but dropped out when his more boisterous personality proved to be incompatible with the organization. John, however, ranked in the top 20 percent of his senior class and was a quiet and avid outdoorsman and hunter who dreamed of a future as a geologist. His teachers viewed him as a quiet, conscientious boy interested in chess, fossils, antique guns, and the outdoors. Although a quiet student, John was a contributing member of his class. One teacher noted his inquisitive and conscientious nature. After a test, he frequently questioned his teachers about the answers he had gotten wrong.

Taking a cue from his industrious parents, John worked in a supermarket after school and still managed to complete homework assignments from his calculus course and other advanced classes. He worked about 25 hours a week from Sept 13, 1969 to March 13,1970, as a stock boy at A&P Supermarkets on Elm Street, refilling bins of fruits and vegetables. The assistant manager at the A&P considered John a steady worker: "If you asked him to do something, he wouldn't even reply, he just went ahead and did it." John's employer commented that "some of the youngsters will grumble or complain about having to leave the shelves and go outside with a package or to collect the carriages. They'll say it isn't their turn or that they're too busy. But not John; he just dropped what he was doing and did whatever he was asked." His boss noted that John was so quiet that when his turn came for a coffee break, he would just go off in a corner, sit down and remain silent for 10 minutes.

Nick Pia, John's driving instructor, described John as "a relaxed kid" who talked mostly about a Boy Scout career. He added that John Rice mentioned the fun he had while on a canoe trip in Canada and a scouting jamboree in Arizona. "He talked mostly about Canada and the deep woods there and how much he would like to camp there." Some of the boys that John Rice went scouting with said he was "as strong as a bull, but feared physical injury for himself." William Pickering, his Scoutmaster in Troop 45, said that Rice never did display fits of temper but "once in a while he'd get a little rough with the younger boys."

One boy, Bob, who became friendly with John during a Scouting jamboree, described himself as being a "fat little butter ball" at the time. He felt a connection with Rice because both boys had been made fun of. He found John to be very nice, someone you could sit down and talk to.

Stephen attended this same jamboree and, according to Bob, "He drove his classmates' nuts." Bob's being "a little butter ball" made him a good target for Stephen's bullying, name-calling, and threats. When Stephen threatened bodily harm, Bob went to John Rice to ask him to get Stephen to lay off. John Rice took care of the matter.

John Rice also came to Bob's defense in another instance. One day during the jamboree, a pine-cone fight broke out between Rice's troop and a group of Boy Scouts from Chicago. The fight became unfriendly and Bob started to take some serious hits from one of the Chicago boys. John Rice immediately went to Bob's aid, restraining his attacker.

John Rice was well thought of among the Boy Scouts – no one in the Scouting organization made fun of him. He was a teacher for the other boys and a helper for the adults.

John loved the outdoors and didn't limit his activities to Boy Scouting; he was also a member of the YMCA Scuba Team, and won marksmanship badges through YMCA activities. He loved to go camping, hiking, and fishing. John became known as a marksman with a rifle, but although he was only several months away from obtaining his Eagle award – the highest award attainable to a Boy Scout – he had never received the Marksmanship Award in Scouting. John's accomplishments in his senior year of high school assured his getting into a good college. He was inducted into the New Canaan High School Honor Society and was about to earn his Eagle Scout honor. Scoutmasters considered the remaining work practically a perfunctory exercise for John and they were prepared to award him the badge of the Eagle rank.

Despite his achievements and confidence in the world of Scouting, there was another side to John. On the day in November 1970 when John was to be photographed with the rest of the students who had been inducted into the National Honor Society, he didn't show up for the photo. Many felt this was a deliberate move on his part, for the shame he felt over his terrible case of acne.

John, a quiet loner, was unlike Stephen, who had more friends and did poorly in school. Halfway through his junior year, he still struggled to finish some sophomore courses. Mainly interested in cars, Stephen spent hours working on the two old, small, unregistered Nash Metropolitan wrecks that were propped up on cinder blocks alongside the family driveway. Inside the garage sat Stephen's yellow 1963 Mustang, along with a 1962 Chevy Sedan and a 1968 Oldsmobile Vista Cruiser station wagon parked outside.

Some classmates recall that Stephen was somewhat of a loudmouth and a bully. Some of his frustration came from being taunted by John. Stephen often told his friends of his and John's constant fighting. In one instance, Stephen spent a great deal of painstaking time on a group of mechanical drawings and John tore them to shreds. Although the two boys were known to get into serious fights with one another, John protected Stephen from fights started by others.

Stephen had more friends than John and Nancy did, and many considered him the only pleasant-looking member of the Rice family. Yet he still stood out in a crowd because of his nearly shoulder-length, flaming red hair and his pale complexion. Stephen also acted strangely. After a friend's father told him that he should cut his long hair, Stephen emerged with a crew cut the next day.

In August 1970, the Rice family lost their grandfather, Percy Fitzpatrick, to a heart attack. Edith Fitzpatrick, Janet Rice's mother, had lived with Percy for more than 30 years and she was lonely living alone, so Janet invited her to come live with them. Edith Fitzpatrick was considered to be financially comfortable. Her house in Byram was fully paid for, as were her car and summer home in New Hampshire. There was also some insurance money that she had received upon the death of her husband. She knew the house in New Canaan was very crowded with five persons living there, but she offered to pay the expense of having a bedroom suite constructed in the basement. John Rice, Sr. felt that the arrangement would give the children a closer relationship with their grandmother. She moved into the Rice home in November 1970.

Stephen gave up his bedroom on the main floor to his grandmother. He went upstairs to the master bedroom, which he shared with his father. John and Nancy kept their rooms on the second floor. Janet, in order not to disturb the family when she returned home late at night from her shift the hospital, slept on the living-room couch.

On Friday December 4, 1970 at 1:45 p.m., Mrs. Dorinda Schreiber sat upstairs in her yellow-shuttered home on Valley Road in New Canaan, reading to her daughters. She heard knocking at the front door, looked out the window, and saw a person standing there. When she arrived downstairs, however, she didn't find anyone at the door. She walked into the kitchen to see whether the person had parked his car in the driveway. Mrs. Schreiber saw a four-door tan Chevy in the driveway. The person came around to the back. She opened the door to John Rice, Jr.

John told Mrs. Schreiber that he was looking for Blackmoor Road in New Canaan and asked if she knew its location. Mrs. Schreiber told him she didn't know the whereabouts of such a road and closed the door slightly. John asked if he could come into her home and see a road map. Mrs. Schreiber, suspicious of his purpose, told John that she was sorry, but that she did not have a map and could not let him in. She closed the door. John Rice sat in his car for several minutes and then drove away. John's severe acne, combined with his 6'1" height and 220-pound frame, might have startled any woman who was home alone.

Christmas time in 1970 brought the Rices the usual excitement and anticipation for the upcoming holiday. Early in December, the Rice family put up their Christmas tree and decorated the outside of their home with holiday lights. On Thursday, December 10, John Rice, Sr. rose early and prepared to leave for work. Janet was asleep on the couch, wearing a pink housecoat. She'd fallen asleep with her glasses on, and John Sr. took them off of her. He went into the kitchen, made himself some instant coffee and let himself out the back door. Even at this early hour, the warmth of Christmas permeated the house. On the kitchen counter rested John Jr.'s Christmas list, which he had left for his mother. He had asked for special clothing so that he could keep warm in arctic temperatures. Janet was proud of John; there weren't many parents with a son who had earned high awards in school and in scouting and who was being sought out by some of the best colleges.

The morning proceeded in the same way as all of the others. The Rice family awoke a couple of hours after John Sr. left for work. Nancy dressed for school while Janet, still half-asleep, asked John Jr. to go upstairs and wake Stephen, who hated to get up in the morning. John, the obedient son, listened to his mom and went upstairs to perform the arduous task of getting Stephen out of bed. Both Stephen and Nancy had missed school the day before because of illness and Janet didn't want them to miss another school day. The children usually fixed their own breakfast in the morning but some days Janet would cook and make small talk. Later in the morning, Edith Fitzpatrick would come up the stairs and she and her daughter would have breakfast and talk about the day's activities and the children. Both women were immensely pleased with all of the children, but especially with John.

When John Rice, Sr. returned home at 1:45 p.m., the shades were down, which was odd for that time of day. Janet always opened the shades as soon as she got up. Edith Fitzpatrick's car was gone and John assumed she had gone out shopping. When he entered the house, however, the horror of the scene within was anything but ordinary. As he entered the living room, he first saw Janet lying on the sectional couch with a hatchet sticking out of the back of her head. It was buried so far into her skull that only the very back end of the blade was visible. Blood coated her hair and had dripped to form a large pool behind the sofa. A seven-inch decorative knife, which had previously hung on the wall above the couch, stuck out of her chest. Although blood had flowed onto the front of her pink night coat and arms from this and another stab wound, John couldn't help but focus on the hatchet buried in her skull. In horror, he pulled the bloody knife out of his wife's chest and threw it on the floor.

Nancy lay naked on the stone slab in front of the fireplace, alongside the couch near her mother. She was lying face up and her wide-open eyes were fixed on the ceiling. She had been strangled with a man's necktie, which was still around her neck. On her left breast was a large bite mark; someone had bitten her hard enough to leave a perfect dental impression.

John Rice immediately called the police. The first time he spoke with an operator, the call was so garbled that he hung up and dialed a second time. When he got the operator, he told her about an emergency that had occurred at his home. He cried frantically, "Oh my God, please send someone immediately. My wife has been knifed and my children are dead. Please, God, send someone here!" The operator notified the New Canaan police.

John Rice went to his wife and tried to take out the hatchet that was embedded in her skull. He was unable to pull it out, though he struggled to remove it with both hands. He then went to Nancy and slapped her in the face in an attempt to stimulate a sign of life.

He stumbled to the master bedroom where he found another horrible scene. Stephen lay in bed on his side, drenched with his own blood. Spatters of blood covered a good portion of the ceiling, headboard, walls, and floor. The entire double bed was soaked in blood. Stephen's head bore numerous large, gaping hatchet wounds that exposed bone and brain matter. Rice turned Stephen over to see his full face, but blood masked the boy's features.

He looked to John Jr.'s empty room, came back downstairs, and looked again at the scene about him with disbelief. A few moments later, he heard moans coming from the basement room where his mother-in-law, Edith Fitzpatrick, slept. He ran downstairs and found her in an unconscious state on her bed, lying on her back with her eyes open. Her head and face were covered in blood, as were the ceiling and walls. She, too, had a gaping wound in the back of her head. The blood-covered hammer used in the attack lay on the floor alongside her bed. John Rice ran upstairs and outside; within seconds, the police arrived.

All available units from the New Canaan Police Department responded. Patrolman Andrew Vitti arrived first after being called on the radio to respond to the scene. John Rice, Sr., in his bloodstained shirt, quickly ushered Patrolman Vitti into the house, crying, "Come inside, come inside, my wife has been murdered." Vitti checked Janet, Nancy, and Stephen for any sign of life, with no luck. Edith Fitzpatrick, however, still had a weak pulse.

Patrolman Vitti called for an ambulance and had Edith Fitzpatrick rushed to Norwalk Hospital by two police officers who stayed with her until she died at 6:05 p.m. She never regained consciousness and the officers were never able to question her. Doctors discovered that a pacemaker had kept her alive after the attack.

Upon arrival at the Rice house, New Canaan Police Chief Keller immediately dispatched detectives and police officers to question neighbors who could possibly offer information that would be helpful in the apprehension of the killer. There were two gun racks containing a number of shotguns and rifles on the wall of the Rice living room and a number of shotgun shells were found strewn about the floor. Chief Keller noted several empty places on each of the gun racks hanging over the fireplace and he asked John Rice, Sr. if there had been guns in the vacant spaces. Rice replied that a 12-gauge shotgun and two rifles were missing from the racks.

He said one of the missing rifles was a .22 caliber while the other was a 30-30 caliber rifle. Nearly all of the ammunition was missing from the drawer where Rice kept it. Police also noted that the women's handbags and Stephen's wallet were empty. John Rice, Sr. told police Janet and her mother usually kept considerable amounts of cash in their wallets. Rice also pointed out that his wife kept emergency money in one of the jars in a kitchen closet. Police found the lid of the jar on the table; the jar itself was empty.

Chief Keller stated to the press that John Rice, Sr. had arrived home from work to find that the inside of his house resembled a butcher shop. He described the scene as "one of the bloodiest murders in New Canaan's history." Keller termed the interior of the home as having the appearance of a slaughterhouse, with bodies strewn in the living room and two bedrooms. Another officer described the home as a "bloodbath."

John Rice, Sr. was brought to police headquarters for medication and questioning. Chief Keller contacted the Connecticut State Police, and several men immediately arrived on the scene. Detective Gene Ready phoned Lieutenant Ralph Scott and, in shock, said, "You are not going to believe what happened. We have got an entire family murdered."

Ralph Scott immediately arrived to question John Rice, Sr. and discovered that John Rice, Jr. was not at home. John Sr. assumed that John Jr. might still be at school.

When police learned that John Jr. was active in Scouting, Chief Keller sent men to search Camp Brown, a wooded area in New Canaan where John Rice, Jr. went camping during the summer months. One officer commented, "We just don't know yet, he could have been abducted." Police questioned a couple of the boy's school friends, but they had no idea where he had gone.

As the police questioned the Rice's neighbors, they found that people viewed the Rices as being a very close family. Though the family lived in the house for 10 years, neighbors hadn't seen much of their comings or goings. The police found no sign of forced entry or indication that any of the victims struggled with their assailant. Several of the family members were in nightclothes when they were found, indicating that the killings had occurred around breakfast time.

In November of that year, a new state law had gone into effect, which put the chief medical examiner in charge of medical examinations of all homicide victims in the entire state. The police and news media waited for over two hours for Chief Medical Examiner, Dr. Elliot M. Gross to arrive from Middletown, where he had been called to check on the case of a college student who had died of a drug overdose.

Dr. Bernard Peterson picked up Dr. Gross in Milford and sped him to the scene of the murders. In the meantime, Dr. Cody, the New Canaan medical examiner at the scene, made a preliminary investigation. He pronounced the victims dead and scheduled an autopsy on each victim for the next morning at the Norwalk Hospital. Dr. Cody stated that from his investigation he believed the victims had been dead for four or five hours.

Chief Keller said that the probable murder weapons – a blunt-headed hammer, a short-handled ax, and a long-bladed decorative knife – were found near the bodies. Keller said he believed this indicated the killer used weapons that were handy and cast them aside as he moved from victim to victim. The state police set up videotape machines and photographed every room in the house. This case became the first one in the history of the nation in which police used videotape to record evidence in a murder.

State police tightened security around the Rice house while dusting for fingerprints. Police were stationed in front of the house and others directed traffic smoothly past the ill-fated home as curiosity seekers slowed down in their cars for a look. Police identification experts dusted the interior of the house for fingerprints as well as dusting the knife, ax, and hammer that were used in the murders.

As neighbors and pressmen waited outside, at dusk, a timed switch suddenly turned on the Christmas lights, startling the onlookers and making visible on the porch a neatly-piled stack of white birch logs, waiting to be fed to a holiday fireplace. Police hastened to find a switch to turn the lights off again.

The doors of the two-car garage, which connected to the side of the house, were open and two cars were visible inside. Another family car was found in the driveway and the Nash Metropolitans were parked on the side of the driveway. The sixth family car, a tan Chevrolet belonging to Edith Fitzpatrick, was missing.

The police dispatched an alarm via the teletype and "hotline" that connected area police departments, declaring that John Rice, Jr. was wanted for questioning in the homicides. John seemed to have left the house in his grandmother's tan 1966 Chevrolet. A pistol, a 16-gauge shotgun, and a sum of money were missing. When asked if John Rice, Jr. was the prime suspect in the case, Chief Keller replied, "We sure would like to be able to question him for a few minutes."

Soon police and residents began suspecting John Rice, Jr. His friends reported seeing him on Wednesday evening, the day before the murders, and that he had seemed his usual self. They didn't believe he was capable of performing such a dastardly crime.

Nick Pia, John's driving instructor, said that he found it "Almost impossible to believe that he would have done anything like this...I was shocked– assuming he did it –I just couldn't believe it due to the fact he was such a gentleman."

At first, police only sought John for questioning but, by noon on Friday, the day after the murders, Chief Keller considered him a suspect. Police also were not discounting the possibility that he too might have been a victim.

Connecticut policemen searched several campsites in the New Canaan area, operating on the theory that Rice may have attempted to camp out as he had done on several prior occasions in connection with his Scouting activities. Police also had authorities in New Hampshire check on a cabin that belonged to the family.

As police intensified their search for John Jr., the switchboard at New Canaan Police Headquarters lit up constantly as newspapers from several states sought information and friends of the family and community members volunteered their services in helping the police.

Shortly after 8:00 p.m. on Friday, a teletype message reported that New Hampshire authorities had checked the area near the cabin and found no tire tracks or footprints.

The New Canaan police issued a nationwide alarm. "We've got to catch this guy," said Chief Keller. A woman informed police that she had passed the Rice home Thursday morning at 10:00 and saw Edith Fitzpatrick's tan Chevy in the driveway at that time. She remembered the fact so clearly because she had lived in the Rice's neighborhood several years ago and made it a point to look at the house whenever she passed through the area, because she had always thought it was so charming.

Despite searches and leads, John Rice, Jr. was still nowhere to be found. One officer commented, "I find it hard to believe that the car has not turned up. John could be almost anywhere, but someone must have seen the car. You don't hide a car like you would a person."

Police again questioned a distraught John Rice, Sr. for several hours in an effort to obtain information about John Jr. At the police station, officers answered hundreds of phone calls, most coming from the news media. Several high school students came forth offering information. Two boys appeared at the desk on Friday and said they had clothing belonging to Stephen, which he had left in a car.

The bodies of the four murder victims underwent extensive autopsies conducted by Dr. Elliot Gross. The killer had imbedded the ax so deeply into Janet Rice's head that if Dr. Gross hadn't removed it carefully, her head would have split in two. Gross confirmed that the victims were murdered some five to seven hours before the arrival of the police at 2:00 p.m. He estimated the time of death at about 7:30 a.m. Neighbors said they heard no commotion that morning.

On Friday night, as falling snow hastened darkness in New Canaan, an unmarked gray station wagon moved up South Avenue, turned into the driveway of Franklyn Hoyt Funeral Home, and backed into the garage. The door closed automatically and the four bodies were removed for embalming.

Late that night, a lone New Canaan Police Officer stood guard near the garage of the Rice home with a revolver in his holster and a loaded shotgun propped against the garage. He explained the shotgun, saying, "We don't know who we're dealing with. The shotgun is loaded; I'm not taking any chances."

Children who had made fun of John at school were afraid for their own lives. One Boy Scout made sure his home's doors and windows were bolted and he slept with a firearm by his bed. A friend of Stephen's who lived a block and a half away from the Rice home slept outside of his parents' bedroom. It was as if a monster was on the loose.

Two days later, on December 12, police officially charged John Rice, Jr. with the murder of his mother, grandmother, brother, and sister and issued a warrant for his arrest. Chief Keller welcomed FBI agents assigned to the case to aid the tiny force of detectives who worked 18 hours a day looking for Rice. The New Canaan Police Department was strained to the limits during this period, despite augmentation of units from the State Police. If Rice had indeed left the state, the FBI forces would hasten the time in which the police would locate him.

Chief Keller depicted John as more than an accomplished Boy Scout on the verge of making Eagle rank. He stated that John Rice, Jr. "has an extraordinary talent to survive in the woods...in any type of weather." The search for John was being pressed in

New Hampshire, where his grandmother owned a summer cottage, and in New Mexico where he spent several weeks during the last two summers at Boy Scout Jamborees. The police even set up a stakeout around Edith Fitzpatrick's vacant house in Byram with the thought that John might be using it as a hiding place.

The 13-state hunt for John Rice, Jr. extended throughout the New England states up to the wooded areas of upper New York state. Rice, an expert woodsman, was believed likely to seek the safety of a heavily wooded area to avoid apprehension.

Police issued a bulletin saying that John Rice, Jr. was believed to be armed and dangerous. Rice's expert marksman titles in both rifle and handgun use added to the danger. Police continued questioning John's friends and relatives with the hopes of getting a live lead as to where young Rice could possibly have gone into hiding. The police searched every Boy Scout camp in Connecticut, as well as those in nearby New York.

The weapons used in the killings were fingerprinted and each showed prints belonging to members of the family. The determination of whose prints were last placed on the weapons was difficult to ascertain.

On the evening of Saturday, December 12, as Dorinda Schreiber sat watching the evening news, she saw a report on the Rice murders and recognized John Rice, Jr. as the man who had come to her home a week earlier asking for directions. In shock and disbelief, she phoned the New Canaan Police and told them of her encounter with Rice. Two days after the murders, there remained no clue as to his whereabouts.

one could understand why John Rice, Sr. would support his murderous son. Rumors and speculations circulated throughout town. Could Rice have been in on the murders with his son? Or was it simply that John Rice, Sr. now felt that he couldn't bear to lose his only remaining son, despite the fact that this son had killed the rest of the family? Or did Mr. Rice harbor some deep-seated guilt for John's behavior? Whatever the reason, John Rice, Sr.'s actions toward his son were viewed by the townspeople as bizarre as the murders themselves.

Shortly after John Rice Jr.'s arrival at the police station, arrangements were completed for his arraignment the next morning at Norwalk Circuit Court. John went through the normal legal proceedings, including fingerprinting, photographing, and formally being arrested and charged with murder.

A dentist by the name of Dr. Lester Luntz arrived at headquarters and police asked John to bite into an apple. He was not to bite off a piece of the apple, just bite into it. By this method, the dentist took impressions of John's mouth. Jerrol Silverberg protested, but Chief Keller prevailed and the police proceeded with the test. Silverberg advised John that it would be best if he quietly submitted to the wishes of the police.

John did remain very quiet indeed. He sat on the edge of his bunk for a long time with his head down.

The next morning in court, John Rice, Jr. sat calm and unblinking between two police officers as he looked around the courtroom, waiting for the proceedings to begin. His father sat quiet and alone in the section for spectators. After the judge entered, court officials beckoned to Mr. Rice and he went forward to stand beside his son. Only about a dozen people, including newsmen, sat in the courtroom. John Rice, Jr., dressed in a baggy tweed suit, a white shirt with rumpled collar and no tie, with his arms hanging stiffly at his side, silently endured the five-minute court proceeding. The judge asked John if the arrangements were satisfactory to the defendant and he answered, "Yes."

The prosecutor informed the court that the charge was murder. Next the judge recited a litany of constitutional rights. Jerrol Silverberg asked for and was granted a continuance of the case on the grounds that he hadn't had enough time to confer with his client. At the conclusion of the proceedings, John Rice, Sr. touched his son's arm and spoke to him quietly, offering a few words of encouragement before John Jr. was escorted out of the courtroom by police.

Court officers walked John Rice, Jr. through the prosecutor's office and out the back doorway while his father moved into the lobby of the court where he allowed photographers to take pictures. Police drove John Rice to the Bridgeport jail and placed him in temporary "administrative segregation" for his own protection. Guards later commented that Rice gave them no problems.

Jerrol Silverberg stressed to the court that John Rice, Sr. was "behind his son in the entire proceedings." He described John Jr. as "very emotionally upset" and in need of serious psychiatric help. He viewed this as the core issue. John Rice and his father agreed that the best thing was to plead guilty by reason of insanity. John Sr. felt that John Jr. was mentally ill and needed to be institutionalized. John Jr. assured Silverberg that he needed and wanted this help. While townspeople gossiped about John Rice, Sr.'s support of his son, Jerrol Silverberg felt that the elder Rice showed good judgment in wanting his son placed in an asylum.

Phil Swaim, who at the time was Jerrol Silverberg's partner, handled Janet Rice's and the estate of Edith Fitzpatrick and began to work on the probate matters involved. All of the lawyers involved in the Rice case remarked how hard it was to believe that John Sr. stood by his son and was willing to do anything for him. Phil Swaim viewed John Sr. as a good-hearted slob and felt rather sorry for him.

During this time, the crime scene at the home was taped off and John Sr. pestered the police about when he could move back into the home. Police thought it odd that he wanted to go back to the house, and indeed that he was in such a hurry to go back. His actions continued to baffle the police and more gossip circulated concerning his surprising behavior. When John Sr. did move back into the house, he tore out the blood-soaked carpets and replaced them, had the walls painted and lived in the house until shortly before the trial.

On Thursday, December 17, 1970, the judge at the Bridgeport Superior Court charged John Rice, Jr. with murder in a bench warrant, which superseded the earlier murder warrant from the circuit court and brought the case under jurisdiction of the higher court.

At the request of the State's Attorney, the Superior Court Judge signed a warrant charging John Rice with murder. Although Norwalk Circuit Court had already charged Rice with the crimes, the new warrant transferred the case to the higher court, which saved time in bringing Rice to trial. Had the move not been made, circuit court officials expected to eventually give the case to superior court anyway. Under Connecticut law, a superior court grand jury has the power to decide whether a murder indictment should be handed down. Another arrest took place, this time at the Bridgeport Correctional Center, where John Rice, Jr. was being held without bond.

Jerrol Silverberg reacted by bringing in as his co-council the best-reputed criminal lawyer in the state of Connecticut: Theodore Koskof of Bridgeport. Koskof had been co-counsel when Black Panther McLucas stood trial on capital charges in the 1969 slaying of another Panther, Alex Rackley. McLucas was convicted only of the least serious charge against him – conspiracy to commit murder – and sentenced to 12-15 years in prison.

Rice's attorneys requested a hearing before the Superior Court Judge to determine whether Rice was deprived of his

Constitutional rights when he police arrested him on December 18th on a bench warrant. They filed a motion maintaining that Rice was deprived of a hearing before circuit court as to whether the case would be transferred from that court to juvenile court. They explained that persons 16-18 years of age, charged with criminal acts were allowed a hearing at circuit court to determine whether the case should be transferred to juvenile court. They added, however, that the few cases they heard about concerned larceny, armed robbery, violence, and aggravated assault. The request by Rice's attorneys would be the first of that nature pleaded in the state of Connecticut.

In January 1971, however, Bridgeport Superior Court Judge ruled that Rice would go before a grand jury. Rice's lawyers argued that the case should not be heard because Rice was a juvenile when he committed the slayings, and therefore juvenile court should try him. The defense team filed for a temporary injunction against the grand jury hearing. The judge noted that the lawyer's plea was "ingenious but not persuasive," and ruled that the power of the circuit court to transfer jurisdiction is a "discretionary, not a mandatory power," and that the judge involved had the power to transfer the case to superior court.

John Rice was born in the spring of 1953, which placed him well into his 18th year when he murdered his family. The juvenile court will sometimes assume jurisdiction over persons who have yet to reach their 19th year or 18th birthday. John had celebrated two birthdays in the Bridgeport Correctional Center and was, at the time of these court proceedings,19 and in his 20th year.

Another issue Rice's attorneys questioned was the admissibility of John Rice's dental impressions being brought into evidence against him. In the ruling, the judge said that Rice submitted voluntarily in the police station to having his teeth examined, and decided to allow the impressions admitted into evidence. Attorney Jerrol Silverberg testified that he objected to the taking of dental impressions because it might force John Rice to possibly incriminate himself, in violation of his Constitutional rights. But, Silverberg also testified that he had advised Rice to cooperate with the dentist.

At the time of the murders, Connecticut had the death penalty and, if the state found Rice guilty, he would have faced life in prison or the death penalty. At the grand jury hearing, John Rice, Jr. pleaded innocent to the four first-degree murder charges against him for killing his brother, sister, mother, and grandmother. Silverberg requested that Rice be tried by a panel of judges as opposed to a jury. The defense team felt that this would give John Rice the best chance of being found guilty by reason of insanity, which would help him to escape the death penalty and life in prison and instead spend his years in an asylum, where his lawyers felt he belonged.

CHAPTER SEVEN

THE TRIAL

John Rice's trial began on April 18, 1972 – sixteen months after he committed the murders – in Bridgeport Superior Court before a three-judge panel. State's Attorney Joseph Gormley first put on the stand the police officers who responded to John Rice, Sr.'s call the day he discovered his family murdered.

Patrolman Andrew Vitti, who had arrived first at the scene, described the locations of the bodies and the condition in which they were found. At the conclusion of Patrolman Vitti's testimony, State's Attorney Gormley introduced photos of the crime scene as evidence. The photos included pictures at a distance and close up to each of the victims.

Next, Gormley summoned Detective Sergeant Eugene Ready to the stand to identify the weapons found at the crime scene. Ready stated that he arrived at 2:05 p.m. just as paramedics were carrying Edith Fitzpatrick out of the house. He then confirmed elements of the scene and identified the murder weapons: a knife, a claw hammer, and a small hatchet. These were introduced as State's evidence.

Attorney Gormley asked if any fingerprints were visible on the weapons. Sergeant Ready answered that there was a slight image on the knife but nothing elsewhere. He stated that the rough surfaces of the weapons thwarted efforts to obtain fingerprints from them.

Next, Sergeant Ready described where he found Nancy's clothing. He stated that two days after the murders, he found Nancy's sweater vest, white blouse, and brassiere hidden among pieces of wood and paper in a closet next to the fireplace in the Rice living room. The bra was torn. Behind the sofa in the living room, he found a purple skirt and a pair of underpants that were also Nancy's.

Ready testified that there was a shotgun on the rack in the living room and other rifles found in the defendant's bedroom, and that there were numerous ammunition boxes and shells found in John's room on the bed, along with a rifle.

Attorney Gormley pointed out that the murder weapons were household items. The murder knife had hung in its scabbard near the fireplace in the living room. The family kept the hammer in a kitchen drawer and John had displayed the Boy Scout hatchet on a wall in his bedroom.

Next, Gormley called Lieutenant Scott to the stand; he testified concerning the evidence he obtained from the Arkansas police and his interrogation of John Rice. The Fort Smith police had turned over a .22 caliber pistol, a .22 caliber rifle and a .25 caliber automatic pistol, together with ammunition, that they said they found in Rice's car. As far as he knew, Fort Smith police had not had a warrant to search the car. Lieutenant Scott stated that Rice barely talked during the interrogation, giving no explanation about his actions other than how he found himself in Arkansas. John Rice had awakened in his car, stiff and shivering, unaware of what had happened. The last thing Rice said he remembered was sitting in his room watching television about 10:00 p.m. on December 9, 1970.

Lieutenant Scott disclosed, too, that he had written a memorandum December 17, 1970, referring to the fact that Jerrol Silverberg had objected to the taking of dental impressions. It was at this point in testimony that the defense reminded the court of another memorandum written by Lieutenant Scott describing his meeting with the defendant December 15, in Fort Smith, Arkansas, where John turned himself in.

The statement given by John Rice was as follows: "I woke up in my car about 20 miles outside Fort Smith after having a dream that I was falling down stairs. I looked at my watch calendar and discovered it was December 14. I was out of gas and a woman helped me get some. I thought my parents would be worried about me and had probably called the police. So I thought the best place for me to go would be to the nearest police station."

The last thing in the world Mrs. Lockey Reed, the Rice family's neighbor, wanted to do was to testify against John Rice. The fact that these murders took place across the street from her had caused her enough distress without her having to become involved in the case. For months after her testimony, she sought psychiatric help and counseling. Doctors gave her medication to help her cope with her heightened anxiety.

In court, Mrs. Reed testified that she has seen John Rice leave the house at about 10:00 a.m. and get into his grandmother's car. She said she didn't notice anything unusual about him and that he drove away in the beige Chevrolet sedan. Mrs. Reed said she did not actually see John Rice coming out of the door or the house, but simply heard him slam it. She assumed from this that he had been in the house, but she said she could not be sure.

When the State's medical examiner, Dr. Elliott Gross, took the stand, he testified to his examination of the bodies and set the time of death between the hours of 4:00 and 8:00 a.m. He confirmed the causes of death for each of the four victims, described the wounds and noted that human teeth made the mark on Nancy's left breast. Dr. Gross added that he found a piece of plastic wrapping paper approximately 22 by 18 inches inside of Nancy's mouth. He said that she suffered a fracture of the small bone of the larynx during strangulation. When Dr. Gross described the details of the wounds to Janet Rice, he stated that the knife pierced her heart.

John sat expressionless in court and listened without emotion to the gruesome details of the murders. His father sat next to him and they talked amiably during the recesses and smiled at each other. John Rice, Sr. leaned against his son during the day as though by this bodily contact he was signaling that he supported him and loved him. Neither took the stand.

State's Attorney Gormley next read aloud the statements given by John Rice, Sr. on December 10 and 12, to save him from testifying. Mr. Rice's statement revealed his whereabouts during the time the murders were committed as well as remarks he made directly after the killings. John Rice, Sr. said that he extracted a knife from his wife's chest when he found her dead in the living room after returning from work at about 2:00 p.m. on December 10. He tried with both of his hands to extract the hatchet from his wife's head, but it would not budge. Rice said that he had slapped his daughter's face in an attempt to stimulate a sign of life.

Gormley identified the hatchet as belonging to John Rice, Jr. and testimony revealed it had hung in a leather case, on which the following words were inscribed: "John Rice Troop 45 Ram Patrol" This referred to John's Boy Scout troop. The other murder weapon, like the hatchet, belonged in the house. Police found no sign of forced entry into the home.

John Rice, Jr. listened attentively to all the testimony but did not change expression when photographs of the bodies were passed to the judges for examination. John followed with his eyes the passage of the photographs down the bench as each judge looked at them.

The judges admitted into evidence impressions and photographs of John Rice's teeth. Rice bit his sister on her left breast just before or after he strangled her. The tooth marks remained the key piece of evidence that the state had which tied Rice directly to the killings. The other evidence was circumstantial.

The defense tried to deride the scientific accuracy of the testimony of Lester Luntz, a dentist from Hartford who took silicone impressions and color photos of the bites on Nancy's breast and matched them to impressions and photographs he had taken of John Rice's teeth. Dr. Luntz identified himself as lieutenant surgeon with the state police as well as a "forensic odontologist" specializing in identification through teeth. He possessed several years of experience on an international level with denture identification. He identified forensic odontaology as a fairly new science and gave lectures on the subject at the Armed Forces Institute of Pathology in Washington, DC. He did not know of any formal course in the science in the United States. A student learned the subject by association with four or five experts living abroad. Dr Luntz named them and said he conferred with them at length on various occasions.

Dr. Luntz stated, during an hour of questioning, that the mark on Nancy's left breast was made by John Rice, Jr. Luntz offered this conclusion after a lengthy description of the means by which he obtained photos and measurements of the bite mark on Nancy's body and compared them with impressions taken from John's mouth. He displayed an articulator device used to obtain models of impressions, and several transparencies that he had used for comparison. Dr. Luntz showed the court that the defendant had a pronounced lower jaw that extended beyond the upper jaw in a way that made the upper teeth crooked in the shape of a "W" or an "M." Dental impressions taken of John Rice, Sr. were also mentioned, but the court ruled they weren't necessary.

The defense attempted to suppress Dr. Luntz's testimony and asked the three judges not to admit the dental impressions into evidence because the dentist had examined Rice's mouth without the consent of his attorney. Attorney Koskof, noted that the first counsel in the case, Attorney Jerrol Silverberg, denied permission for the impressions at police headquarters that night. He said Dr. Luntz took them at the direction of the New Canaan Police, despite

Silverberg's protestations that the action might violate Rice's Constitutional rights. Koskof argued that the inspection of John Rice's mouth without the consent of his lawyer was an invasion of privacy. He distinguished the entrance into a bodily orifice, like the mouth, from taking fingerprints or photographs of the face, which police can take without consent of the defendant. Angry that he was not being heard, Attorney Koskof cried, "How hard can you object to something like this? Does it have to come to using force?"

Koskof argued that new testimony from Lieutenant Ralph Scott provided the opportunity for a new review, and offered the Schmerber vs. California case of 1966 as the legal precedent for the court to allow suppression of the dental impressions. In that case, he said, the court found that search warrants are just as important where intrusions into the body cavities are concerned as they are in the search of dwellings. "Inferences to support such search should be drawn by a neutral and detached magistrate instead of being judged by the officer engaged in the often competitive enterprise of ferreting out crime," said the court. "The importance of informed, detached, and deliberate determination of the issue whether or not to invade another's body in search of evidence of guilt is indisputable and great."

Several months earlier, Superior Court Judge Samuel Tedesco had denied a defense motion that the tooth impressions and photographs be suppressed. Attorney Koskof asked that the judge overturn Tedesco's ruling. The motion was denied.

State's Attorney Joseph Gormley told the court that Dr. Luntz's credibility as an expert witness was at the heart of the State's case against Rice. Jerrol Silverberg doubted the dentist's credentials in forensics and viewed his science as quackery. Upon cross-examination, Silverberg discovered that in the area of Dr. Luntz's dental forensic expertise, he had only taken a three-hour seminar. Gormley later told a reporter that he never found any report of an American trial in which the prosecution attempted to link a defendant with a murder through tooth marks. Koskof agreed with Gormley that he did not know of such a trial. Despite the protest from Rice's attorneys, the tooth mark evidence was allowed. It was the only evidence the State had to link John Rice to the murders.

Doctors Thomas Detre, chief psychiatrist at the Yale School of Medicine, and Johnathan Himmelhock, the associate director of the Acute Inpatient Division at Yale, testified for the defense. Dr. Robert Miller, director of Fairfield Hills Hospital in Newtown, Connecticut testified for the prosecution. Miller concurred that Rice suffered from a severe mental disease on December 10, 1970 that left him incapable of controlling his impulses. Dr. Detre described Rice's mental disease as a severe compulsive disorder. According to the doctors, John Rice developed an obsessive compulsion to kill because of severe psychotic decompensation. Rice lacked substantial capacity to conform his conduct to the requirements of the law.

During an interview on December, 14, 1971, John Rice, Jr. disclosed to his psychiatrists that he was seized with such overwhelming impulses to kill that he often climbed into his car to drive around the neighborhood. This maneuver had been successful in ridding Rice of violent impulses in the past, the doctor explained. Six days before the murders, however, the impulse became so intense that John pulled into the driveway of a house at 496 Valley Road, New Canaan – the home of Mrs. Dorinda Schreiber – with the intent to kill whoever was inside. He knocked on the door and, during the long wait for an answer, apparently regained enough control to ask for directions instead of forcing his way in. Referring to the woman's intelligence in not letting him inside, Dr. Detre said, "that's probably why a murder didn't occur that day in New Canaan." Dr. Thomas P. Detre, told the court that a murder would have occurred, had it not been for Dorinda Schreiber's suspicions.

The three psychiatrists, all of whom had talked with John Rice and his father, agreed on Rice's insanity and painted the composite picture that John Rice, Jr. was an extraordinarily placid and well-behaved young man. But, as time went on, he had become increasingly isolated, socially. He had very few good friends. For as long as 14 months before the tragedy, intensive foreign anxiety – producing thoughts of murder and mayhem – thrust themselves on his consciousness. The thoughts were fragmented at first, and not disabling in frequency. Rice could shrug them off by turning his attention elsewhere.

Some six to seven months before the murders, John Rice "seemed to be increasingly overwhelmed with the urge to kill somebody," Dr. Detre said. It was not an urge that focused on any specific persons or persons. About six weeks before the murders, these thoughts began to occupy from one-third to one-half of John Rice's waking hours. At first he had been able to control them. Now they seemed overwhelming. Dr. Miller said Rice was sufficiently frightened to feel that he needed a psychiatrist, but he did not tell his parents. Perhaps he feared to reveal his bloody thoughts to them.

The psychiatrists claimed John's concentration began to deteriorate and he became more isolated and lonely. Images of violence and mayhem began to fill John's mind. His schoolwork suffered; his life seemed to deteriorate. After a particularly bad period, he would become exhausted and thoroughly confused and restless, and experience bad dreams, some of them violent. The psychiatrists said that Rice described the murders in detail and though he had been aware of the wrongfulness of the acts, he could not control himself. They also told the judges that Rice's condition was unchanged since December 1970. His conduct was "depersonalized," meaning he was aware of what was going on, but detached himself from it and would not become involved.

Dr. Detre said that John was unsure as to whether he would have killed his own father if John Rice, Sr. had been at home the morning of the murders.

John was sexually immature. In late adolescence, when most boys become sexually active, John had no experiences or outlets. When he killed his mother and sister, he partially undressed them out of curiosity, because he had never seen a naked woman before. "John apparently had no social contact with the opposite sex, like he thought Stephen had had," said Dr. Miller. "John was an isolated individual who evidently had absolutely no outlet for his sex drives. When ever sex intruded into his thoughts, he apparently drove them out."

He resented his brother Stephen, who was much more popular and had an active social life. John showed no remorse for his actions, rather, he seemed to find relief in them. "He was incapable of actively relating to other people," Dr. Miller said. "He was among people but never with them."

Dr. Miller said that John Rice's impulse to kill on December 10 had been triggered by his younger brother Stephen. Referring to an April 3, 1972 interview with John, Dr. Miller said that Janet Rice had asked John to go upstairs and wake Stephen, who normally was the last one up in the Rice household on a school day. Dr. Miller said that, during the interview, John had indicated a distinct jealousy toward Stephen.

Miller noted that while Stephen was a vibrant individual who got into a lot of trouble both inside and outside the family, he also had an outgoing personality that had gained him many friends. This was in direct contrast to John's more quiet nature and solitary inclinations. "John resented Stephen's social success," said Dr. Miller. "So it isn't hard to understand that when he went upstairs that morning to wake Stephen and got the answer 'get lost,' it was enough to trigger manifestation of his impulse to kill." The possibility that Stephen was the first victim gained substantiation from the fact that Nancy was evidently already clothed and downstairs at the time mayhem began in the Rice household that morning

Dr. Miller said John admitted to removing Nancy's clothing and also gave a description of how he methodically washed up after the murders, and stocked his car with enough food, ammunition, and guns to subsist by himself in the wild. "It was his intention in some vague way to go to the southwest part of the country and live off the land," noted Dr. Miller.

Referring to the interview with John Rice Sr., Dr. Detre said, "The father said there were no danger signs in John that were obvious, that would have led him to seek psychiatric counseling." In fact, John Rice, Sr. said the family had considered having Stephen see a psychiatrist.

All three psychiatrists concurred that the murders still seemed unreal to John Rice, Jr. They said that though he had been left in a daze, he had also experienced a sense of relief. All three also agreed that Rice was still in the same detached state as 16 months earlier when he committed the murders. "I suppose he is able to look back on these acts," said Dr. Detre, "but there is still no sign of remorse."

Dr. Himmelhoch observed that John had suffered more confusion of thoughts in the morning as compared to other times of the day. The three doctors said that John Rice had not suffered severe impulses since the murders, but that those impulses could certainly return. While they would not say just how long it might take John Rice to rehabilitate, they indicated it would take a long time. State's Attorney Joseph Gormley made the long road to recovery clear by saying, "It will be a long time before I could be convinced by any amount of medical testimony that John Rice, Jr. will be ready to take his place in society again without harm to himself or to the community." John's attorneys declined to make a statement, but indicated they were not in disagreement with Gormley.

The state rested its case Tuesday after presenting six witnesses. The defense moved immediately for a dismissal on the grounds that a prima facie case had not been made out. The three judges took a 15-minute recess then returned with a unanimous decision to override the motion.

Attorney Michael P. Koskof asked for a dismissal on several grounds, including the fact that the state had failed to connect the defendant to three of the murders and had managed only circumstantial evidence in connection with Nancy's death. "No motive has been shown," he said. "There has been no evidence presented to prove conclusively that John Rice, Jr. was present when these events occurred. There is no evidence to show his fingerprints on any of the weapons or his hair in the vicinity of the victims. The State hasn't shown a modus operandi. This is all poor speculation."

Koskof went on to note other obvious loopholes in the testimony of the state's witnesses including the fact that the state's principal item of scientific evidence was the matching of John's dental impressions to a human bite mark on Nancy's left breast. He even dismissed this evidence by noting that the state's witness represented was absent. State's Attorney Joseph Gormley admitted perfunctorily that his case "relied almost entirely on circumstantial evidence."

The next day in court, the judges began deliberations and, in 20 minutes, handed down their decision. At 11:57 a.m. Wednesday, Judge Harold Mulvey, presiding judge of the three-judge panel that tried Rice, asked him to stand. Judge Mulvey told John Rice, Jr. that he had been acquitted unanimously of murdering his family because he was suffering from a mental disease at the time. Rice looked at Judge Mulvey with the same lack of emotion and concern he had displayed during the two-day trial.

Rice was taken to Fairfield Hills hospital in Newtown, Connecticut. The judge ordered hospital authorities to file a report on Rice's mental condition within 60 days, on whether he was still a danger to himself and the community. The State's Attorney would review the findings, and he had the right to offer rebuttal evidence to any positive discoveries made by the doctors.

On receipt of the report, the judges would reconvene, presumably for the purpose of sentencing Rice to an indefinite term in a state mental institution for the criminally insane. Had the court not found John Rice, Jr. guilty by reason of insanity at the time of the murders, he might have faced the death penalty for four first-degree murder charges.

CHAPTER EIGHT

THE RICE HOUSEHOLD

Many in town remained shocked that John Rice killed his family. The newspapers highlighted John Rice's achievements and portrayed him as a polite, bright student who emotionally snapped. The school's principal, James O. St. Clair, called Rice "a superior student" who was in the top 20 percent of his class. He also noted that Rice's special area of interest was fossils and environmental studies. Rice's physics teacher, Stanley A. Twardy, felt that Rice was only an "average" student who did not speak up very often in class. Rice's former physics lab partner, John Madigan, told newspapers that John "was a very intelligent kid, but he wasn't very outgoing...I don't think he ever went out on a date in his life. He always seemed very nice to me."

In 1970, the story of the boy next door who "lost it" sold newspapers. These newspaper reports misled the public into believing that John Rice's life had focused on his wonderful achievements. Many reporters never researched John's home life and his relationship with his family. Criminals and killers generally do not have the discipline to reach goals. John Rice never reached his either. He never achieved the Eagle rank in Boy Scouting because he murdered his family members.

To some, the Rice family seemed like a normal, quiet family. Lockey Reed, the neighbor who lived across the street from the Rices for six years, said, "They were a quiet family." She noted that Stephen and Nancy seemed friendlier than John, who kept to himself.

Other neighbors, however, said that they heard shouting and swearing going on inside the house, but never gave it much thought. One neighbor commented, "They kept to themselves and we ignored them."

The family didn't fit into New Canaan; not because of their working-class status, but because of their strangeness. Not one member of the family possessed charisma, style, or good looks. In a town like New Canaan where preppy, well-groomed appearances are the norm, the Rice family stood out. The Rices didn't fit in in New Canaan, but it is unlikely that they would have fit in anywhere. Sadly, because of the family's strangeness, when John Rice, Jr. killed them, there didn't exist a soul who was willing to fight for the victims.

The three Rice children all exhibited behavior that bespoke of something seriously wrong going on in their home. This was evidenced at the murder scene. When Janet Rice was murdered, she had been asleep downstairs on the couch because her husband had been sharing a bed with their son Stephen – an arrangement that was quite bizarre.

Stephen was described by all of his classmates as a loudmouthed, obnoxious bully who liked to aggravate people and pick fights. He had exhibited these traits from childhood. His grades were also poor. John was a loner who displayed disassociation and violence from early childhood. Both boys were described as having serious tempers and extremely foul mouths.

Nancy exhibited the behavior of a very disturbed and depressed teenager. All of the Rice children were described as dirty-looking because of their messy and greasy hair, but Nancy seemed to take the lead in looking filthy and unkempt. She spoke in a squeaky voice and exhibited painfully shy behavior. When it came time for her to give an answer in class, she had a hard time getting the words out. Even among her own friends, Nancy didn't talk much and seemed withdrawn.

When Nancy's closest friend visited the Rice home at the age of 12, she felt very uncomfortable. Stephen constantly picked on and teased his sister. Though John was quieter than Stephen, he also picked on Nancy and both boys repeatedly punched Nancy in the arm. When the boys were not punching Nancy, they were beating each other. Nancy's friend had never been exposed to this kind of violence but, since she had no older brothers herself, she told herself that this was how older brothers might treat younger sisters. Nancy once commented that John's punches really hurt. The unattended children had the run of the house and freely acted out their violence on each other.

One day, Nancy and her friend were sitting in Nancy's room, looking through a book on sex education that they had just received from their teacher. John Rice, Sr. entered and asked Nancy to leave and go get something for him. Mr. Rice sat down next to Nancy's friend, picked up the book and began reading it. He then placed his hand over her pants and rubbed her vagina briefly.

Another incident occurred later that summer. John Rice, Sr. picked up Nancy and her friend after they had gone shopping. Nancy's friend sat in the center of the car's front seat, next to Mr. Rice; Nancy sat closest to the window. As they were driving home, Mr. Rice grabbed his daughter's friend's hand, put it over his crotch and squeezed it. The young girl froze. Mr. Rice then put her hand down his pants and squeezed it over his penis. He didn't say a word and after doing this for a few moments he stopped. After this incident the young girl broke off her friendship with Nancy and never went to the Rice home again.

Mr. Rice might not have thought twice about doing this in front of Nancy because he might have been sexually abusing her. If so, this may have explained her weight problem, greasy hair, depression, and insecurity.

If Nancy was widely regarded as withdrawn and depressed, then Stephen tipped the scales the other way by coming across as a bully. In one instance, eight-year-old Stephen and nine-year-old John were walking home from school when they came across a six-year-old girl. Stephen repeatedly hit the girl over the head with his metal lunchbox. An adult ran to her aid and the boys ran off. Later, the girl's father confronted John Rice , Sr. about the incident. When the door closed behind him horrible screams were heard as John Sr. whipped the boys.

Statistically, by age 24, 60 percent of identified bullies have a criminal conviction. Bullies usually come from middle-income families that don't monitor their children's time or activities. Parents of bullies tend to fall to one of two extremes: they are either extremely permissive and allow their children to get away with everything, or they are physically aggressive and abusive. A bully bullies because he or she needs to be in control of situations, and because he or she enjoys inflicting injury on others. They are generally not committed to their schoolwork and show a lack of respect toward their families. Sometimes bullies lash out because they are angry about something. Sometimes someone in their life is bullying them. They might be hurting from abuse they received in the past or maybe grew up observing those around them using violence as a means of settling differences. Stephen's reputation as a bully is evidence of major dysfunction in the Rice household.

John Jr. and Stephen shared an odd relationship. John envied Stephen and unleashed on him the greatest of his fury the day of the murders. John chopped into Stephen's face and skull nine to eleven times. Yet, schoolmates recall John being very protective of Stephen. "John always stuck up for his brother," said one boy, "and his brother got picked on a lot." Another said of John, "He'd really raise hell if anyone picked on Steve."

In one instance, when Stephen was in the seventh grade and John was in the eighth, Stephen had been harassing a boy named Nick during a Boy Scout meeting. A fight ensued. But, like a bear coming for its prey, John emerged, grabbed Nick and Stephen by the clothing on their backs and threw them apart. Stephen yelled to John, "I can fight my own battles," and started swinging at John, who briefly fought back, the two of them swearing at each other all the while. Nick can still recall the crazed look on John Rice's face as he broke up the fight, and his almost superhuman strength.

One neighborhood boy, a young violinist named Bob, endured six years of being tormented and bullied by Stephen before deciding to fight back. He learned some fighting techniques from a friend and, one day when Stephen tried to bully Bob, Bob beat him up. Not long after this incident, Bob was walking in the hallway at the high school when suddenly Stephen and John Rice emerged. The brothers threw Bob on the ground and kicked him until he could barely pick himself up.

Bob's battles with the Rice brothers didn't end there. Shortly after the ambush, Stephen saw Bob on the street and began yelling at him from near the end of the Rice's property. Bob challenged him to come out of his yard. Stephen walked out to Bob and a fight began – once again, Bob was the winner. His victory was short-lived; John Rice, Jr. came out and beat Bob badly in the road. Bob weighed about 235 pounds and he was nearly six feet tall, yet he says John Rice threw him around as if he were a rag doll. Bob commented that it was as if John had an on/off switch. "Here he had no friends, never talked to anyone, was real quiet," Bob remembered. "He was achieving a lot of things at school, but when the switch turned on, John Rice acted like and had the strength of someone on angel dust or crack."

The beating left Bob terrified of John Rice; he felt fortunate that John hadn't killed him. When he was asked about the murders, Bob felt that there was a contradiction in John's lifelong protection of Stephen culminating in Stephen being the most brutally murdered that terrible morning. Bob felt that John "didn't want anyone else to beat up Steve, *he* wanted to...vengeance is mine."

In another instance, a high school boy named Evan retaliated against Stephen's aggression and slapped him. Stephen told John of the incident. Evan was sitting on the floor in one of the hallways at the high school when, without warning, John Rice walked and kicked him in the face. He continued to kick Evan while in a "trance-like rage." Another student and a coach who happened to walk by tackled John Rice to the ground, ending the attack.

At the time, there existed in the basement of the high school a shooting range for the rifle team. When both John and Stephen joined the team, the club's officers petitioned the principal of the school and asked that the Rice brothers not be allowed on the team. They were afraid that one Rice brother would get angry and start shooting the other one. Their fighting was so frequent and notorious that the rifle club's officers really felt that the Rice brothers were a danger. The principal stated that the Rice brothers would not be denied membership on the team because he did not believe any student should be prejudiced against or denied access to any of the school teams. The student officers were so concerned about the Rice brothers that they broke the club's rules and filled their magazines with as many bullets as they could hold, instead of the standard one round per magazine that was allowed at practice. They wanted to be prepared in case of a Rice-provoked shoot-out.

Classmates recall that Rice brothers fought constantly, with John usually beating on Stephen. One schoolmate recalled John Rice pulling his car alongside Stephen's, getting out, grabbing Stephen by the hair and dragging him out of his own vehicle.

Some students noticed John Rice's hot temper as early as his grade school years. In one instance, when John was about 11 years old, an eight-year-old boy threw a rock at him. He grabbed the boy by the heels and swung him around violently while laughing hysterically. The boy's terrified mother screamed out of her window for John to put her son down. When he ignored her cries, she phoned the police, who came along with John Rice, Sr. Everyone shook hands and made amends, but the boy's mother never forgot the horror of that day. The boy never forgot either, and he refused this author an interview, out of fear of John Rice.

While Stephen's actions were obvious and easy to read, as they characterized rebellion and anger, John turned inward. Although John appeared quiet, temperate, and amiable, these traits masked John's disassociation with the real world as violent thoughts consumed him. John's violent side emerged enough times to indicate that a serious problem existed.

Mr. and Mrs. Rice both covered up the family's dysfunction. Janet Rice spoke of her wonderful husband and her intelligent son John. John Rice, Sr. talked as if all within the home was quite normal, despite the fact that the early morning hours found Stephen in bed with him, and his wife downstairs on the couch. John Rice, Jr., the sole surviving member of that household, refuses to speak to anyone. Thus no one will ever know exactly what took place in that house to produce a killer, a bully, and a despondent, sad girl but one can speculate.

Five months after Mrs. Rice gave birth to John she became pregnant with Stephen. As John turned 14 months old Janet gave birth to Stephen. Not quite a year later she conceived Nancy. Most likely Mrs. Rice ignored John as she dealt with her pregnancy and Stephen's birth which occurred when John began toddling. His resentment for Stephen might have started early in his life as he felt abandoned by his mother when she looked after baby Stephen. Overwhelmed by the three small children, Janet Rice probably dealt with them violently as well as verbally abused them in her frustration. Mr. Rice most likely reinforced this behavior by issuing his own violent discipline and verbal abuse of the children. There is no telling how far the abuse went or what horrible acts of child abuse were enacted on the children by the parents in their anger.

Each attempted to control them by this behavior. The Rice kids reenacted the violence onto each other, evidenced by John continuously beating on Stephen and both brothers hitting their sister with such regularity. Resentment and rivalry fueled their violence.

The marital relationship between Mr. and Mrs. Rice was most likely strained. When Stephen gave up his room to his grandmother when she went to the home to live, Stephen moved into his father's bed.

The papers reported Mr. Rice saying that Mrs. Rice slept on the couch so that she would not disturb Mr. Rice when she came in late, yet she thought nothing of 15 year old Stephen sleeping in bed with his father and the disturbance he might cause his dad? Mrs. Rice might have slept on the couch because of the animosity she felt for Mr. Rice. The stress of the children being so close in age, the failure of the restaurant which caused financial pressure and Mr. Rice's unrestrained behavior toward women and young girls added to their arguments.

When Mr. Rice grabbed Nancy's friend's hand and pulled it into his pants as they sat in his car, this was done in eye's view of Nancy. Dad most likely sexually abused Nancy and didn't care if she witnessed his abuse of her friend. The lack of boundaries and respect exhibited reveals the symptoms of their inward dysfunction as individuals and as a family unit. It can never be known how far Mr. Rice went in acting out his deviant sexual behavior and if this included either of the boys.

Mrs. Rice distanced herself from her family and emotionally abandoned her children in the process. She was a nurse who worked the later shift and left to go to work after the kids came home from school. When her schedule allowed her to be with her children she chose to take college courses instead. The abandonment magnified John's rage, Stephen's anger and Nancy's insecurity. The angered relationships created constant chaos in the home. John's good grades which probably came natural to him and his participation in the Boy Scouts gave him a sense of normalcy. These achievements might have given him recognition from his mother. Amidst Stephen's out of control actions and Nancy's depression and shyness John appeared to be the emotionally normal one in the family.

John experienced such emotional turmoil from his awkward appearance combined with the lack of proper nurturing, mistreatment, and chaos that he inwardly wanted to explode. He obsessed about killing and developed an obsessive disorder because of the constant anxiety he experienced from the trauma and his spirit literally broke in two and birthed his killing fantasies. In this home environment, John developed no self confidence and was emotionally immature. After killing his family John felt no remorse because there was no remorse to feel over the people who broke his spirit and groomed him into a sociopath.

CHAPTER NINE

A RICE-MOUNT CONNECTION?

When John Rice murdered his family, police and reporters questioned if there was any connection between the Rice slayings and Mary Mount's murder. Newsmen, many residents and even some policemen noted the "striking similarities" and rumors began to circulate that John Rice had killed Mary Mount. Mary was killed by a hard blow to her head, which is also what killed three of the four victims in the Rice household. Although John used four different weapons, in three of his victims the attacks were mainly to the head area.

The Mount family had lived only a few doors away from the Rice family until buying their home on Willowbrook Lane. Five months before Mary Mount's murder, the Mount family lived four houses down from John Rice. John used to walk by the Mount home on his way to school and his other activities. He could have easily seen Mary while she was out playing in her front yard.

In Mary's case, a man was seen in a white or light-colored car. John Rice drove a light colored Belaire when he first began to drive. Although he didn't obtain his driver's license until June 18, 1969 – three weeks after Mary Mount's abduction – Nick Pia, John Rice's driving instructor, noted that John already had some "pretty good" driving skills when he began his lessons. Janet Rice left for work as her children were returning home from school. John Rice, Sr. left for work so early in the morning that he often napped during the day, leaving the Rice teenagers to do whatever they pleased. John Rice could have easily driven off in his father's car without his father being aware of it.

Mrs. Cogswell, the witness at Kiwanis Park, noted that the driver drove at a normal rate of speed, which may have indicated that the killer was detached from his actions. Psychiatrists noted that Rice disassociated himself from his crimes.

Although many New Canaan residents believed that John Rice killed Mary Mount, several police officers didn't believe Rice fit the profile of someone who would abduct and murder a child. Chief Keller didn't see a connection except for the fact that the Mount family had rented a house about half a block from the Rice home on Millport Avenue. Chief Keller termed the possibility of John Rice's involvement "extremely remote." Those within the detective bureau who felt that Rice's crimes bore no resemblance to the Mount murder believed that John Rice's crimes were an act of rage against his family. They believed that a sexual offender or someone who primarily killed young children had murdered Mary Mount.

Although Chief Keller didn't consider Rice a strong suspect, he attempted to question him. Rice's attorney, however, refused to allow John to be questioned in the Mary Mount homicide. Chief Northcott of the Wilton police encountered the same response, and thus John Rice was never interrogated in the Mary Mount case.

In 1972, when the Rice trial was heard, the study of serial killers hadn't even begun. It wasn't until criminal profiler John Douglas took over as chief of the operational side of the Behavioral Science Unit at the FBI, in the late 1970s, that this began to change. Rice didn't show signs of insanity, but he exhibited several traits common in serial killers. He admitted to having fantasies about killing and also admitted to scouting for victims. His lack of remorse for his crimes revealed that John exhibited the characteristics of being a sociopath, i.e. someone who has no regard for life or the suffering of others. Experts who study serial killers also learned that killers don't always use the same method when they kill, they don't necessarily stick to the same type of victim, and many serial killers begin killing at a young age. Although John Rice exhibited these characteristics, a good deal of his anger was directed at his family.

Many within the New Canaan Police Department believed that the convicted Harold Mead was the best suspect for Mary Mount's murder. Mead did kill children by a blow to the head, but he murdered in the New Haven area. Although rumors of his being a milkman and an ice cream truck driver in the New Canaan area made it into newspapers, these rumors were never substantiated as fact. Mead worked at his father's service station and was able to use the cars that came in and out of the station; this might explain the reason that the white car used in the murder was never found.

Mary Mount was last seen in a remote area at the back of a secluded park, known only to town residents. There was a window of about 10 minutes in which she was left alone. The killer was most likely parked in the lot and saw Mary all by herself. He was familiar enough with the park to drive back to where Mary played, but not familiar enough to know that the Cogswells' home was back there. Many residents who had lived in town for years and who used the park on occasion were also unaware of the Cogswells' home being at the back of the park, because the house appeared to be part of the concession area.

Mary Mount's killer most likely had been to the park on other occasions. John Rice knew the park; he was a Boy Scout and the Scouts used the Kiwanis facility and it was in walking distance to his home. Rice was also a fisherman and behind the park were ponds that boys used to fish in. Harold Mead is also said to have been familiar with parks, but he was mostly familiar with state parks.

Mead is a small, soft-spoken man who could easily fool his victims, whereas John Rice's looks alone would frighten anyone.

Rice also possessed little skill in being able to interact with people; he was basically a loner. If John Rice abducted Mary Mount, he would not have tried to coax her; he would have most likely grabbed her quickly.

Mary Mount's killer drove her to a remote area in Wilton, Connecticut, six miles away from the site of her abduction. Wilton police officials speculated that Mary Mount would have had to be taken to the reservoir by somebody who knew the woods well. Although police felt that the links between the two cases were slim and rather circumstantial, Wilton Police Chief Northcott stated, "One out-of-the-way place might be a coincidence. But that a stranger would find two of them is too much to believe." Chief Northcott said that there is no doubt the killer was someone with a reasonable knowledge about the Norwalk reservoir area. He said there are four ways to get into the section of the woods where Mary Mount's body was discovered. He said the most obvious, and shortest, route is to enter at Old Huckleberry Road. The single-lane, poorly maintained dirt road off Rt. 106 became a causeway bisecting the reservoir.

Old Huckleberry Rd. off Rt. 106 is located between Wilton and New Canaan. It looks like an old road that would lead to nowhere, and woods surround the narrow, hilly, windy road but it is a road a local fisherman would know about. Above the reservoir, the road leads to a good fishing pond known as Rock Lake. New Canaan and Wilton police have, over the years, driven into this area, which resembles the great forests of Maine, to continually chase couples in cars out of this section. Police term the area a "lovers lane."

John Rice, Jr., as a skilled woodsman, camper, hunter, and Boy Scout, knew the Kiwanis Park and reservoir areas. Rice admitted that when he had the urge to kill he would take drives and this helped to diminish the urge. On one of those drives he ended up at the Schreiber home on Valley Road, which is the route one must take to go from New Canaan to the Wilton Reservoir.

Although authorities favored Harold Mead, the townspeople believed John Rice murdered Mary Mount.

International criminal profiling consultant Greg Cooper examined the Mount case and provided a criminal profile. Mr. Cooper had served as Chairman of the Utah Criminal Tracking and Analysis Project (UTAP), and Chief of Police and Civil Defense Director of Provo, Utah. Prior to that position, Cooper worked for the FBI from 1985-1995 in various investigative and supervisory positions within the Seattle, Washington division, Los Angeles, California division, and at the FBI Academy Training Division in Quantico, Virginia.

Cooper co-authored the Crime Classification Manual, a landmark book that classifies homicide, arson, and sexual assault. He has consulted internationally with law enforcement agencies on over 1,000 cases.

Greg Cooper's childhood mirrored those of many of the killers he now studies. Greg was born to two alcoholic parents who divorced when he was six years old. Greg witnessed a lot of fights. His mother slept on the couch with an iron to protect herself.

The Coopers lived in Las Vegas, where Mrs. Cooper worked as a waitress. One day the police came to the door and told Greg's mother they had warrants for her arrest because of unresolved parking tickets. Mrs. Cooper initially told Greg to sneak out and tell the manager of their apartment that she was not at home, but she decided against it and told him to stay. Greg's mother was arrested, and he was also taken to the police department, where his mother was forced to spend a night in jail. A detective took Greg home with him for the evening and treated him very well, which minimized the impact this traumatic event had on him. This left Greg with conflicting feelings. There was anger towards the police officer who took his mother away but, on the other hand was the detective who nurtured him and took him home.

During Greg's eighth year, his mom remarried a man who left his wife and three children for her. Greg's stepfather suffered guilt about having left his family, and he and Greg's personalities were nothing alike. Soon jealousy and animosity developed between the two of them; they both competed for Greg's mother's attention.

Greg's stepfather and mother also drank together, which led to fights that often became physical. By the time Greg was 14 years old, he took it upon himself to interrupt physical fights between his mother and stepfather. When Greg was 17, he joined the Mormon church, which brought stability and structure into his life.

Greg's mother encouraged him to become a lawyer, but he wanted to go into law enforcement and went to work in a Provo police department. His chief became his mentor, and he ended up graduating valedictorian from the police academy. Eventually he went into undercover work, setting his sights on becoming a police chief, which he attained. From there, Greg went to the FBI, where he quickly climbed the ranks. Ultimately, however, Greg felt that he was limited inside of the Bureau and left because he believed that he could be more effective acting as a consultant, teaching law enforcement agencies worldwide.

According to Greg Cooper when examining the Mount murder, the killer abducted Mary and did not lure her. "This blitz approach reveals that the killer has no charm about him; he has poor interpersonal skills. For some reason he has been out to Kiwanis before and he has been to both places. He was out there for a legitimate reason, he might have been an employee who went out there or he went out there for stalking purposes."

Cooper commented that this crime was impulsive and the killer did not necessarily plan it. Mary was playing by herself and the killer was opportunistic. He agreed with the earlier authorities that probability was good that the person in the white or light-colored car committed the murder. Cooper added that Mary's murderer had a fantasy life, and would probably be attracted to someone close to his own age but, because of his inadequacies, he would not be able to attract someone his own age.

Cooper said that the abductor drove slowly enough not to attract attention to the vehicle; this shows sufficient control. Somehow he controls Mary – she has got to be afraid. The shoe left behind suggests a scuffle – there was force used in her abduction. After some struggle, the killer gets her into the car, where he can control her.

The killer might be someone who worked at both the park and the reservoir. Mary could have been killed in the car. Cooper theorized that at the moment of the abduction after the killer threw Mary into the car her screaming would have unnerved her abductor who would have hit her in the head to quiet her. He might have hit her with a hammer. The wound on the side of her head was a huge hole. The way Mary's body was left, it is very feasible that she was assaulted and dumped there. If she was killed with a rock, it would have been near the body. If Mary was still alive when she was brought into the woods, the killer would have had to bring the murder weapon with him as well. Cooper maintained that a killer like Mary's wasn't that organized.

An unorganized killer is one who is socially immature and sexually incompetent. Such killers don't follow the crime in the news and the murder is usually spontaneous, with the crime scene being sloppy. These killers leave the body where it falls and leave behind the weapon as well. The violence is sudden and there are no restraints or torture. Younger offenders might remove the clothes of the victims and touch the sexual organs, but will not damage them.

Organized killers, on the other hand, are outgoing and articulate. They like to follow the crime in the news, and might kill again to keep the story in the news. They like attention and enjoy the feeling of superiority. They will often torture their victim before killing, enjoying the power it gives them, and will return to the scene of the crime to gloat. This type of killer plans everything and targets a stranger. They like to maintain control over everything, they torture their victim, remove the body from the scene of death and dispose of it. They may take souvenirs of the crime, including body parts. Some killers exhibit both organized and unorganized characteristics.

Cooper stated that "the ways in which the Rice family members were killed and the nature of the wounds signified John Rice, Jr.'s hatred of his family. He hated his brother Stephen inside and out, and unleashed his greatest fury on him.

With Stephen's blood on him, and carrying the axe to use on his mother, he went downstairs. When he saw his sister in the kitchen he strangled her. This murder is less about anger; it's impulsive, opportunistic. He bites her on the breast, which shows anger, but in removing her clothing he reveals sexual inadequacy and curiosity. John attempted to hide Nancy's sweater, blouse, and bra in a closet. According to Cooper, "this was a pathetic attempt to conceal what he had done. Nancy was not the focus of the assault, she was the aftermath. John may have been embarrassed by what he did with his sister, so he hid her bra and sweater. He might have come to a realization that his attack on Nancy was beyond what he had in mind. With no regard for her life and as if mocking her he crumpled up a large piece of cellophane and stuffed it in her mouth, deep into her throat as if she were a garbage receptacle. According to Cooper, Rice knew the meaning and this would be considered a signature.

The same hatchet John used on his brother, he left in his mother's head, which, to John, was the final act. He knew he had to do something about his grandmother, and went downstairs to finish the situation off.

It is odd that Stephen was found sleeping in his father's bed. Part of John's anger towards Stephen might have been because it bothered him that John Rice, Sr. and Stephen slept in the same bed. John followed the natural inclination to be his brother's protector. He was able to appear normal by standing up for his brother. Who knows what John fantasized about, concerning what was going on in his father's bed? Whatever goes on in the mind of such an offender can be completely delusional. What he perceives as going on, *is* going on. After murdering his family, John may have found relief and never wanted to kill again."

Sadly, Mary Mount's murder remains a mystery and no one might ever know who really killed her, except for the killer himself. Based on Greg Cooper's opinions, John Rice, Jr. fits the bill more completely than Harold Mead does, because Mead lured his victims and Mary Mount was abducted rather than lured. Thanks to criminal profiling, we can have more clues into these mysteries and more understanding as to who killed Mary Mount and why.

If John Rice killed Mary Mount, based on what we know about his urges to kill, he might have driven around while having his permit and having been entertaining his killing fantasies. He probably drove around both to get rid of the urge as he stated to psychiatrists and inwardly hoped that an opportunity would present itself. John drove to the park to pull himself together and there in front of him in the distance was this child playing all alone. John couldn't resist the temptation. He drove to the sand pile and grabbed her and threw her in the car and acted out his fantasy by hitting her as hard as he could in the head with a hammer or other hard metal instrument. Several months later he felt the need to kill again and each time he got in his car he drove around looking for victims. If no victims presented themselves he would drive back home.

One month before John Rice killed his family his need to kill became so great that he pushed himself to knock on Mrs.

Schreiber's door. The woman never let John into her home so he left. One month later he killed his family.

Many of the town's people who lived at that time believe that John Rice killed Mary Mount. Her grave rests in a small section of New Canaan's Lakeview Cemetery. Up on a hill in the same cemetery rest the graves of Edith Fitzpatrick, Janet, Stephen, and Nancy Rice.

CHAPTER TEN

JOHN RICE FREED

The outcome of the Rice case shocked New Canaan residents almost as terribly as the murders themselves. To many, the case epitomized the failures of the criminal justice system. These injustices began with the headline, "Young Rice Inherits Victim's $60,000.00." When Jerrol Silverberg's colleague, attorney Philip Swaim, handled the Fitzpatrick estate and realized that John was in line to inherit the estate, the big question was, could a killer inherit money from his victims? Connecticut state law required that no person judged guilty of first or second degree murder shall inherit or receive any part of the estate of the deceased, but it said nothing of a person found not guilty by reason of insanity when committing such homicides.

Edith Fitzpatrick left her estate to her daughter Janet, who in turn would have shared it with her husband. In the case of Janet dying before Edith, the money was to go to Edith's eldest grandson, John Rice, Jr. The filing of the will disclosed that the inventory of the Fitzpatrick estate came to $58,160. Janet Rice's estate came to a little over $3,000. John Rice, Sr. applied for guardianship over the $60,000 John, Jr. inherited from two of his victims – his grandmother and his mother. The court appointed John Rice, Sr. as probate guardian. The attorneys agreed that young John Rice was the legal heir. The only way John Sr. could get the money was if his son gave it to him as a gift.

Insurance investigators questioned who died first – Edith Fitzpatrick or Janet Rice. If Edith died before Janet, Janet would have inherited the Fitzpatrick's estate and her husband, John Rice, Sr., would have shared the money. During the trial, witnesses and documents established that Edith Fitzpatrick died several hours after Janet Rice, therefore the Fitzpatrick estate went to the eldest grandchild: John Rice, Jr. The money went into savings accounts in New Canaan after Mr. Rice sold the property.

John Rice, Jr. inherited his victims' money and used that money to pay for the legal and psychiatric fees that helped to find him not guilty of their murders. As if this wasn't enough injustice, it was discovered that Edith Fitzpatrick's wounds rendered her brain-dead at the time of the attack. A pacemaker kept her heart beating for the several hours following Janet's death. If it hadn't been for the pacemaker, Edith Fitzpatrick would have been found dead.

When the judges who tried John Rice found him not guilty by reason of insanity and placed him in the Whiting Forensic Institute for the Criminally Insane, many people, including his own attorney, believed that Rice would spend the rest of his years there.

However, only a short time after Rice was admitted to the Whiting Forensic Institute, doctors allowed him to enroll in a community college in Enfield, Connecticut. He was released from the facility almost daily so he could go to school to get an associate's degree in business.

Five-and-a-half years after Rice entered Whiting, a superior court judge ruled that John Rice was "not a danger to himself or others," and should be released from the institution. Freedom made him eligible for the insurance money he had inherited.

Judge Thomas O'Sullivan of Orange, Connecticut signed the memorandum of release after a hearing at which two psychologists and two psychiatrists testified that Rice would not be a danger to himself or to others. Rice had petitioned for release earlier in the year, and three staff members of the Whiting Institute had testified on his behalf. Following the hearing, the State's Attorney's office in Bridgeport Superior Court hired a psychiatrist to review the testimony. Dr. Peszke, the state's psychiatrist, examined John Rice, Jr. on two occasions. Peszke testified that because of John's experience, the possibilities of his indulging in violent dangerous or homicidal behavior again were "very low and possibly lower than the average citizen in the community."

In his two-page memorandum, Judge O'Sullivan said, "The evidence showed that Rice had reached such a point in his progress that Whiting officials had allowed him to leave the institution for overnight and weekend trips for various recreational, social, and educational purposes."

The Assistant State's Attorney, Richard F. Jacobson, stated that Rice "Is 10,000 times improved from the kid we picked up in 1970. He was a vegetable then; he never said a word or gave any indication of emotion. He talks and behaves like a normal person now."

Rice's attorney stated that in the last five-and-a-half years, John Rice had left Whiting Forensic Institute 400 times in his own car. Rice was in the Institute to "ensure that he can cope with society." The attorney claimed that in court transcripts, psychiatrists determined the reason for Rice's insanity in 1970 was based on "inadequate emotional development – his inability to cope with the social pressures of adolescence, and normal anger for that age was internalized." In other words, he just exploded.

Rice's attorney said that John Rice would not return to New Canaan but would continue his schooling at Aspetuck Community College in Enfield, where he had earned an associate's degree.

As if all of these events were not grievous enough for the lost lives of the victims, the State of Connecticut would now protect Rice from his crimes for the rest of his life. Since Rice was found not guilty by reason of insanity, the State of Connecticut erased Rice's files. Wherever John Rice went, he would never show up in any database as having committed murder; he would show no criminal record whatsoever. The police department that apprehended him for his crimes would now be forced by law to offer him protection by denying that any files on him ever existed.

According to Dr. Norman R. Klein, Ph.D., a psychologist specializing in clinical and forensic psychology and an expert witness in criminal, civil, and family courts in State and Federal jurisdictions: "The point of the insanity defense is to explicate people who cannot be held responsible. He did not really get away with murder. Yes, he killed those people. Yes, he is culpable of that, but in the legal system the standard for insanity includes the idea that the person does not know what they are doing is wrong or can't control themselves to conform to what is expected.

It has changed in a variety of ways in the last 30 years, but not fundamentally. To have been released suggests that they had enough exposure to him to suggest that he is not dangerous."

Although this is true in the eyes of the law, in John Rice's case, the insanity defense proved the public fear that those who are found not guilty by reason of insanity end up being freed sooner than those who are found guilty of murder charges. This is not true in every case, and sometimes defendants spend more time in an institution than they would have spent in prison if found guilty.

For example, Anthony Kiristis, an Indianapolis businessman who, in 1977, strapped a shotgun to the head of a mortgage banker who planned on foreclosing on Kiristis's real estate project, was found not guilty by reason of insanity and committed to the hospital ward of the Indiana State Reformatory at Pendleton, where he still remains. Had he been convicted of the charge – kidnapping – or plea-bargained to a lesser charge, he might be a free man today.

Ed Gein, a serial killer from Wisconsin, was acquitted by reason of insanity for the murder, mutilation, and skinning of at least two women in the 1950s. Gein admitted to robbing bodies from graves. He made body parts into ornaments and clothes that he wore to re-create the image of his dead mother. The Hollywood movies *Psycho* and *The Silence of the Lambs* looked to Gein for their inspiration. The State of Wisconsin committed Gein to a state psychiatric hospital, where he remained until his death.

Although these cases exist, horror stories of defendants who were found not guilty by reason of insanity for murder charges and released back into society, only to commit more murders, also abound. In Chicago in 1975, Thomas Vanda stabbed a 15-year-old girl to death. Vanda was found insane and released back into the community in 1976, despite objections from psychiatrists who declared his psychosis was only in remission, as well as objections from the judge and Vanda's own defense council. Three months later he stabbed and eviscerated a 25-year-old woman with a five-inch hunting knife. As the woman lay on the floor, hemorrhaging, Vanda inserted his penis into the open wound in her abdomen and masturbated until he ejaculated into the wound. He was convicted of murder in June 1979 and sentenced to 500 years in the Illinois Department of Corrections. Within a two-year period, at least five Chicago-area murders were attributed to people who had been previously acquitted on insanity pleas.

The case of serial killer Edmund Kemper is also well-known. When Kemper was 14, he shot his grandmother in the head with a rifle and, after wrapping her head in a towel, he moved her body up to the bedroom where he slashed and stabbed her with a knife. When his grandfather pulled into the driveway, Kemper met him at the door and shot him dead. When Kemper was 15, the Youth Authority committed him to Atascadero State Hospital where he became a model patient and was taken under the wing of research director Dr. Frank Vanasek. Kemper became a trusted inmate among staff and was released in 1970. Doctors believed he no longer posed a threat to society, but Kemper went on to kill and decapitate three women. While the head of his third victim rested in his car, he attended a follow-up evaluation by a board of juvenile psychiatrists, where he was declared mentally stable and the record of his double homicide of his grandparents was sealed.

He killed his fourth victim and buried her head in the front garden of his house. He killed two more women, decapitated them, and had sex with one of the headless corpses. Kemper next killed his mother by hitting her in the head with a hammer and cutting her throat until he decapitated her. He took out her larynx and tried to destroy it in the garbage disposal, but it jammed. He told police later, that in death she was still yelling at him. After killing his mother, he raped her corpse and propped her head on the mantel for use as a dartboard. He then phoned his mother's best friend, asked her to come to the house and, when she arrived, he clubbed her over the head, strangled and decapitated her.

He then turned himself in to the police and told them that he no longer needed to kill anymore because all of his rage had been directed at his mother. Now that he finally killed her, he had no desire to kill again. Kemper admitted to cannibalism and also claimed that he had memorized the responses to 28 standardized psychological tests so that he could give "well adjusted" answers. On November 8, 1973, he was found guilty of his crimes and sentenced to life imprisonment in California Medical Facility at Vacaville.

There was also the 1981 case of Robert Nolan, who murdered his 24-year-old wife and her 34-year-old boyfriend. At the time Margaret, Nolan's wife, was going to leave him and seek custody of their four-year-old child. Nolan stabbed Margaret 17 times and her boyfriend 40 times. He was found not guilty by reason of insanity at his trial, and was released a few months later. Sixteen years later, Nolan's second wife filed for divorce after nine years of marriage. Upon receiving notice of this second divorce, Nolan killed his second wife with a shotgun. He then turned the gun on himself.

There are also those high-profile defendants who did not win the insanity defense, among them, Jack Ruby, Sirhan Sirhan, and Mark David Chapman, as well as serial killers David Berkowitz (New York's "Son of Sam" killer), Jeffrey Dahmer, John Wayne Gacy, and Herbert Mullin, who killed 13 people in Santa Cruz, California.

Contrary to public opinion, the insanity plea is used less often than people assume. Wyoming citizens assumed that this defense was used in half of all criminal cases and that it was successful in one of five cases, while statistically it succeeded in only one in every 200 cases. A survey of the use of the insanity defense in eight states between the years of 1976 and 1985 found that although the public estimated that the insanity defense was used in 37 percent of the cases, the actual rate was only 0.9 percent. Although many states do not document the use of the insanity defense, a 1994 survey found that the overall success rate of the insanity defense was 26 percent. This means that of the nine insanity defenses raised in every 1,000 cases, about two will be successful.

After the trial of John W. Hinckley, Jr. who, on March 30, 1981, attempted to kill Ronald Reagan and shot four other men, found Hinckley not guilty by reason of insanity, the public expressed outrage. After the Hinckley ruling, every legislature examined the insanity defense. Congress and some states passed laws designed to toughen standards in insanity defenses. Instead of requiring prosecutors to prove a defendant's sanity, defense attorneys now carry the burden of persuading a judge or jury their clients are insane.

The insanity defense varies in each state. Three states have abolished insanity as a defense. The Federal government has revised its definition of the defense three times since 1950. Some states have also adopted a tougher release system. Such changes in Connecticut doubled the average term acquitted defendants spend in institutions and apparently caused the number of insanity pleas to drop.

In response to the Hinckley case, the Whiting Forensic Institute established the Psychiatric Security Review Board in 1985, a state agency to which the Superior Court could commit persons who were found not guilty by reasons of mental disease or defect. Prior to the existence of the Board, patients were sent to the Department of Mental Health, and a number of them got lost in the system with no supervision. PSRB takes jurisdiction over the acquittees and decides which hospital to send them to, and when they can be released into the community. The Board comprises six members who represent professional expertise in the fields of law, probation/parole services, psychology, psychiatry, victim's services, and the interest of the community.

The responsibility of the committee is to order the supervision and treatment necessary for the acquittee to become harmless to the public. Victims have the right to be notified of all board and court hearings concerning the acquitter's status and they have the right to make statements at any board or court hearing. The hearings are open to the public.

The foremost purpose of the board is public safety. The system would rather err on the side of public safety, as opposed to the rights of the victim. If John Rice, Jr. committed his murders today and was again found not guilty by reason of insanity, with the PSRB in place, he would have remained in Whiting for life. The Psychiatric Security Review Board became a model for hospitals nationwide.

When the Whiting Forensic Institute released John Rice, newspapers reported that he was going to continue at school and get a four-year degree in business. His father moved to New Hampshire, to the vacation home that Edith Fitzpatrick had owned. From there, John Sr. moved to a trailer park, where he lived until he died of colon cancer in 1999. John Jr. had him cremated.

John Jr. moved to Enfield, Connecticut and from there moved up to New Hampshire. A schoolmate saw John at the Massachusetts Big Eastern State National Fair in 1983, with an unattractive young woman on his arm. John seemed unchanged to this person – he had an empty, dead look in his eyes. In 1988, John Rice and his wife Sharon began raising and selling llamas, with Sharon running the show and John acting as helper. The Rices took their llamas to local fairs. John's photos of their prize llamas can be seen in various internet locations. Sharon knitted items from the llama yarn and sold them. Greg Cooper commented that an individual as socially inept as John Rice would prefer the company of a big animal like a llama to people.

John and Sharon will talk about their llamas for hours, but neither of them will address any questions dealing with their pasts. Sharon goes out of the way to protect John; the two of them live mostly like recluses.

When they first moved to their home in New Hampshire and obtained their post office box, John Rice used his wife's last name. Some have speculated that John Rice might have met his wife at the Whiting Forensic Institute.

In 1970, newspapers portrayed John Rice, Jr. as a young man on the road to success, prior to killing his family members. Highlighting his ranking in the top 20 percent of his class, and his desire to go to college and study geology, no one would have imagined that he would have ended up a farmhand.

Although John Rice made himself known as a teenager as a hunter and fisherman, he never obtained a fishing, shooting, or hunting license while in New Hampshire. With age, John Rice, Jr. grew large and sloppy-looking. He still wore his pants too high and his hair in a late 1970s style. His large jowls and hanging receding chin make his features almost unrecognizable. Nevertheless, if one looks closely enough, one can still see the unmistakable underbite and Y-shaped front tooth configuration that left the distinct mark on Nancy Rice's breast.

Although John attends fairs with his wife, he never looks anyone in the eye. His eyes flicker and look off to other directions as he talks. Many who meet him still consider him strange, and his wife is considered odd as well. When John Rice walks into a crowd of people, he still appears as the reporters noted at the time of his trial, "among people but not with them."

CHAPTER ELEVEN

CURED? REHABILITATED?

Can an individual who brutally murders four of his family members at the age of 17, who admits that his mind is occupied with killing fantasies, be cured and rehabilitate? The science of psychology blossomed in the 1960s and 70s, and many psychologists embraced the idea that the criminal was not a bad person by nature, but a product of his environment, and that therapy could aid in healing him. In the 1980s, crime skyrocketed and some of the most horrific crimes were committed by the criminals who had been released from prison into society. The 1990s to the present have brought back tougher sentences, victim advocate programs, and sexual offender public notification lists.

Psychology, in regard to rehabilitation, plays a vital role in the American court system. Judges constantly send less-serious offenders into programs for treatment of everything from alcohol and drug programs, to problems managing one's anger. Many of these programs are known to be successful. When it comes to hardcore violent offenders, however, the picture changes. Criminal experts have come to the conclusion that there is no cure for these individuals.

And so the question is, was John Rice cured? Did he, as he said, never have the urge to kill again once he killed his family? Has he gone on to live his life, never to have murdered again? If that is the case, he has an incredibly rare story to tell; many people would want to know how and why rehabilitation worked for him when it has failed for others. To this day, John Rice, Jr. refuses to speak to anyone concerning any detail of his personal life, so no one will ever know the answer to this question.

John Rice's murder of his family qualified as mass murder. Rice also exhibited some of the characteristics of a serial killer. In admitting that his thoughts were preoccupied with murder, Rice displayed the one thread common to all serial killers: fantasy. John Rice regularly engaged in the fantasy of killing. He told his psychiatrists that his victims could have been anybody; he killed his family both out of rage for them and also for the sake of killing – to fulfill the fantasy. Rice had also admitted to being out on the hunt for victims one week before he killed his family. He also exhibited the traits of a sociopath by showing remorse for his actions or any grief over his murdered family members.

Have there been unsolved murders in the area in which John Rice currently lives? In his book, *The Shadow of Death: The Hunt For a Serial Killer*, Philip E. Ginsberg wrote about the Connecticut Valley River murders, a series of murders that took place along the New Hampshire and Vermont border. Two of the murders took place in Clairmont, New Hampshire, which happens to be where John Rice, Sr. and his wife Janet were married.

On July 25, 1981, 37-year-old Mary E. "Betsy" Critchley was last seen hitchhiking on I-91 in Massachusetts. Loggers discovered her body on August 9, 1991, in a remote wooded area in Unity, New Hampshire. Betsy was fully clothed, missing only her sandals and knapsack.

On Friday, May 28, 1982, at about 4:00 p.m., 76-year-old widow Sylvia Gray finished a tea party at her home with three other women and went to the post office, which was a five-minute walk from her home. She got her mail and returned home. When Sylvia's sister never heard from her that evening or the next morning, she tried calling several times but got no answer. They searched for Sylvia all day Saturday. On Sunday morning at 11:30 a.m., the body of Sylvia Gray was found on her family's land about a five-minute walk from her house. Her body had been thrown headfirst over a small embankment at the edge of a field. Her skull had been beaten in and her throat and wrists were cut. The cuts were non-lethal; the head injury had killed her. Her clothing was undisturbed and there was no evidence of sexual assault. The large, five-stone diamond ring that Sylvia Gray always wore was missing and never found. There were injuries to her left ring finger.

On May 30, 1984, 17-year-old Bernice Coutemache was last seen hitchhiking in Claremont, New Hampshire. Her skeletal remains were found on April 19, 1986, scattered along a brook in a remote wooded area in Kellyville, New Hampshire.

A few months later, on July 20, 1984, 26-year-old Ellen Fried was last seen at a pay phone in front of a small store in Claremont, New Hampshire. The store, located in a poorer section of town, was closed. Ellen's car was found the next day, about three miles from the phone booth, in a secluded area in West Claremont. Her body was found by hunters on September 19, 1985, in a very secluded area in Kellyville, New Hampshire, 10 miles from where the car was found.

One year after Ellen Fried's abduction, on July 10, 1985, 27-year-old Eva Morse was last seen hitchhiking in Claremont, New Hampshire at about 8:00 in the morning. On April 25, 1986, her skeletal remains were found in a remote wooded area in West Unity, New Hampshire. There was no evidence of clothing adhering to the remains or in the area.

Most of these homicides appeared to have been committed with a knife or a knifelike cutting object. These females were each alone at the time of their disappearances and their bodies were located roughly 10 miles from where they last seen alive. All the bodies were found within a 25 mile radius of each other.

About nine months later on April 15, 1986, attractive 37-year-old Linda Moore was sitting in the sun in a lawn chair at about noon. Her shoes were under the chair and her portable radio was playing. Between 12:30 and 1:00, Linda went into her home, where she was stabbed 25 times in what would later be called gross overkill. This murder was linked to the others because it occurred within a 50-mile radius of them.

Six months later on January 10, 1987, 39-year-old Barbara Agnew went skiing in Stratton, Vermont with a friend. She left in a major snowstorm and her abandoned car was found shortly thereafter. Agnew's clothing and ID were found in a Dumpster and blood was found in her vehicle. Her body was found on March 28, 1987, 14 miles from the rest area in Hartland, Vermont, in a secluded area where it was believed a four-wheel drive vehicle must have been used to reach the dumping spot, due to a heavy snowstorm that dropped 18 inches of snow on March 10. Paint chips found on the bumper of Agnew's vehicle were believed to be left from a 1973 to 1978 AMC product Jeep wagon truck.

On August 6, 1988, 22-year-old Jane Boroski, who was seven months pregnant, stopped her car at a local grocery store in Swanzey, New Hampshire, which was closed, and the parking lot was dimly lighted. At 3:00 a.m., an older Jeep Wagoneer, brown with wood-grain paneling pulled beside her. The operator, a white male, 30-40 years of age, assaulted her with a knife when she resisted being pulled from her vehicle. Boroski was stabbed many times and played dead. She was the only victim who lived and survived this perpetrator's brutal attack.

On July 1, 1989, 33-year-old Pamela J. Webb was reported missing from Winthrope, Maine. Her body was found on July 18, 1989, in a wooded area off of Rt. 3 in Franconia, New Hampshire. Oddly enough, the criminal profiler who worked the case stated that this offender was someone who hated his family. The artist's drawing based on the testimony of Jane Boroski resembled John Rice, Jr.

Between July 1988 and April 1989, nine women who were either drug addicts or prostitutes were found dead and their bodies were dumped along Interstate I-95 and Routes 140 and 88 in the New Bedford, Massachusetts area. Two other women were also missing but the bodies were never found. They were also presumed to be victims of the same killer. Three of the murder victims were strangled. This case became known as the deadliest serial killing case in Massachusetts since the Boston Strangler in the 1960s, and was chronicled by author Carlton Smith in his book, *The Killing Season*.

One self-proclaimed prostitute testified before a grand jury that she too had been attacked. but that she had fought the attacker off. She claimed that he also attempted to pick up two of her roommates and that prostitutes in the area had seen him around. The perpetrator of these serial homicides was never found. According to Lieutenant Jose Gonsalves, formerly New Bedford's chief investigator, "These murders still haunt the investigators to this day." He stated that a problem in the investigation was that many of the victims had never been reported missing. Their bodies were hidden well enough so that they wouldn't be discovered. The summer heat accelerated their decomposition. When bodies were discovered, they didn't match the descriptions of those who were reported missing.

By the time the third body was discovered, officials realized these homicides were part of a serial killing. Lieutenant Gonsalves stated that, at the height of the investigation, the serial murders had come to a halt and he believes that at that time the person who was responsible either died, moved on, or was incarcerated for other crimes. This part of Massachusetts is not far from where John Rice, Jr. currently lives.

There are also murder victims who have turned up not far from Rice's farm. In January 19, 1997, the body of 36-year-old

Rosalie Miller was found in the woods in Auburn, New Hampshire. On October 4, 1998, four children went to play in the woods in their back yard and stumbled upon the body of 31-year-old Mindy West with a noose around her neck. She had been missing since July of that year.

Both of these women knew each other; both were from Manchester, New Hampshire and both and had drug problems. The detective who worked the Rosalie Miller case felt that he had a good suspect but there was not enough evidence to bring up charges on the individual.

On August 5, 1993, 10-year-old Holly Piirainen of Grafton, Massachusetts was abducted from her grandmother's house. Holly was a smart girl who wanted to grow up to be a marine biologist. Holly's mother was very security-conscious. She enrolled Holly in karate, and showed her safety videotapes. But, Holly's parents were divorced and her father didn't share the same standards as his wife. He allowed Holly to take her five-year-old brother Zaccary up the road to look at puppies. Zaccary came back, but Holly vanished. All that Zaccary could recall was a sound that detectives believed might have been a van. Two months later, Holly's body was found seven miles away in Brimfield, Massachusetts. Sadly, when the body was discovered, the police contacted Mr. Piirainen, but failed to contact Holly's mother, who learned about the discovery on the news. Holly's murder remains unsolved to this day.

In mid-June 2000, 30-year-old Deborah Melo vanished from Taunton, Massachusetts. Her disappearance was followed by the abduction of 16-year-old Molly Bish on Tuesday, June 27. Molly had just taken a job as a lifeguard and had worked at the swimming pond for eight days when she was abducted. A day earlier, when her mother dropped her off, she noticed a strange man sitting in a white car staring at Molly as she walked around in her bathing suit. Mrs. Bish thought it odd that a man would be lurking in that area at 10 in the morning, when most people are at work. Mrs. Bish was so alarmed by this man that she had a talk with Molly to making sure the girl took safety precautions.

The next day, Mrs. Bish received a phone call from the swimming pond. Molly hadn't shown up for work. When the police went to the scene, they discovered Molly's shoes, radio, and other belongings neatly placed on the ground. There appeared to be a spot where a struggle had taken place, because tree branches were found broken. Molly's first aid kit had been opened but there was no sign of Molly. Despite a composite drawing of the mysterious man, a $100,000 reward, and an exhaustive hunt on the part of the Massachusetts State Police, Molly Bish and her abductor have not been found.

The sad reality is that if John Rice were responsible for any one of these homicides, no one will ever know because of the lack of evidence left at each of these scenes and because of the age of some of the cases. If he were responsible for any of these homicides, the blood of the victims is on the hands of the State for releasing Mr. Rice back into society.

John Rice lives like a recluse, he has gone out of his way in his aging years to remain low-key and keep his name hidden. Although he did take photograph of his llamas and place his name and copyright symbol on them. According to Criminal Profiler Greg Cooper, if Rice was responsible for the Mount murder then he would most likely be killing today, but his rage did appear to be directed against his family and he could have, as he said, found relief after killing them and never had the desire to kill again.

Cooper feels that Rice lives like a recluse because he wants to lose his identity, forget who he is or was in the creation of who he wants to be now; he wants no association to the incident of murdering his family. Rice's crime of slaughtering his entire family ranks, even to bad guys in prison, on the bottom of the totem pole and is viewed with disdain even by hardened criminals.

Serial killers gain notoriety, a sense of legacy, but someone like this who wipes his family out is so contrary to human nature that even the most derelict will look on in disgust. There is no ego-building or notoriety here, such a person is isolated, a social misfit and he does not want to be reminded of who he is and what he did. To the degree that he can, he wants to remain anonymous.

About three years ago John and Sharon left the state of New Hampshire and moved to West Plains, Missouri. Those within the Llama association said financial hardship caused the Rice's to sell their farm and move. Coincidentally, this was not long after this author began phoning John Rice and sending him emails in an attempt to interview him. His wife's website no longer exists and neither he nor Sharon show up in any searches except for their previous work for the llama association. West Plains, Missouri lies close to the Arkansas border , the location John Rice fled to when he first murdered his family. Did financial problems cause Rice to move? Or did he leave New Hampshire as Cooper stated in an attempt to place his past behind him and remain anonymous ? If he committed more murders is he again running to protect himself?

According to Cooper, "His satisfaction or glee might not go back to the family situation. He didn't kill for a sense of power, he had a lot of animosity and anger. Something triggered him to murder that day, there were precipitating stressors. Any victim outside of the family would have been a mere substitute."

Thus Mr. Cooper concluded that if John were responsible for the Mary Mount murder, it is likely that he has killed again, but if he only killed his family and his anger were directed at just them, he might never have needed to kill again.

Rice's secrets might end up dying with him; no one will ever know for sure what went on in his home or in his life after he left the institution. For a time he found himself a safe haven, though, in a rural town that rests on a large lake. His farm was one of several that existed on his road, and his home, which rested close to the road, bore all the charm of a quaint New England farm house. Yet, in the middle of a sun-filled day, the vehicles were all in the driveway, and the shades were drawn, protecting all of the secrets that lie within and possibly behind.

CHAPTER 12

THE WIND CRIES MARY

In the abduction and murder of Mary Mount, the New Canaan police did everything that a police department could do to solve the case. For a small suburban department, they handled the crime as efficiently as they were able and in many areas they went above and beyond the call of duty. In the domains where they lacked manpower or resources, they did not hesitate to phone the State Police and FBI for support. To this day, the New Canaan Police still hold out hope and conduct somewhat regular reinvestigations into the Mount murder, while many other departments disregard their older cases. A majority of the officers treated the Mary Mount crime as if it happened to their own daughter. Mary became their special little girl. The detectives who worked the case served out the remaining years of their career with the goal of finding Mary Mount's killer.

When the Wilton Police Department became involved, conflict began as Wilton investigators refused to share findings with New Canaan police. The case became theirs to solve because Mary Mount's body was found in Wilton. Wilton detectives never disclosed to New Canaan authorities that they discovered Mary's second shoe until years after the shoe was found. The location of the shoe verified the exact path the killer walked that day. The refusal to share information occurs in police work all of the time, because of police policy which affirms that sharing details of a crime is detrimental to the solving of a case. This refusal to share extends to state investigators. Police will leave out various details of a murder to help them catch the real killer. In part this policy exists because of individuals who will confess to a crime they didn't commit. This happened in the case of serial killer Hadden Clark. While incarcerated for two murders, Clark confessed to homicides he never committed. One of them included Sarah Pryer of Wayland, Massachusetts. Clark had read enough in the papers to know many facts about the case, but his confession didn't match the details of the murder. Unbeknownst to Hadden Clark, the Wayland police already had a very good suspect.

There are a myriad of issues with police policy which contribute to the difficulty of solving random murders. One is the jurisdiction problem. When murders occur in different locations, it is difficult to recognize patterns or serial murders. In cases where two departments might join in the hunt for the same killer, so much attention is paid to each department caring for its own case that departments do not collaborate efficiently and help each other. According to several sources, egos are often to blame and the goal of justice for the victim is lost.

Police salaries are paid by the tax dollars of their town or city, and police departments can only perform their function within town boundaries. The 105th Session of Congress passed the "Protection of Children From Sexual Predators Act of 1998," which authorizes the FBI to investigate serial killings if requested by the head of a law enforcement agency with jurisdiction over the offense. While this allows the FBI to aid in an investigation and provide assistance, resources, and guidance to departments, it is still limited.

Presently, the FBI's Violent Criminal Apprehension Program (VICAP) offers a service designed to address this problem. VICAP is a nationwide database that collects and analyzes data from solved and unsolved homicides, especially those that involve abductions that are random, motiveless, and sexually oriented.

Once a case is entered into VICAP, it is compared continually against all other entries with the purpose of detecting signature aspects of homicide and similar patterns of modus operandi. When a serial murder suspect has been identified, VICAP assists the law enforcement agencies with relevant cases by coordinating a multi-agency investigative conference. The problem is, making a report to VICAP is not mandatory and, because the paperwork is extensive, law enforcement officials shy away from making reports. At one time there were 185 questions that needed to be filled out. This number went to 95 and has since been reduced a bit further. Each law enforcement agency has authority to decide if they will participate, so VICAP's database is not extensive.

Another factor that hinders the solving of crimes is lack of hard evidence. The media highlights victorious cases in police work, leading the public to believe that a perpetrator always leaves evidence. In the cases of many abducted children, however, barely any evidence is left behind. Sometimes the little evidence that might be found cannot be linked to any one person. When a killer dumps his victim's body in the woods, by the time someone discovers the body, often little to no evidence remains. Without enough evidence, the police have little to help them search for and apprehend a suspect.

Other factors contributing to a police department's efficiency in solving a murder include budget and time constraints, and legal red tape. Big cities have larger budgets and skilled detectives. Smaller departments that exist on limited budgets do not always possess skilled investigators. Even in cases for which the help of the FBI is enlisted, the Bureau has its limitations as well.

Once the police apprehend an individual, the system does not always work to provide justice. The law that can be responsible for apprehending these individuals can also set them free. In Connecticut, state law helped acquit John Rice of four first-degree murder charges, helped him to inherit his victims' money, and erased his files so that he could not be brought up as a suspect in any other murder based on the murders he had already committed.

Along with the laws, there exists the unpredictability and unreliability of the judicial court system itself. Horror stories abound of criminals who were released too soon or found not guilty, to people who were later released from stiff sentences after DNA evidence revealed their innocence.

Criminal courts are overloaded, hearing hundreds of cases each week. Prosecutors and defense attorneys each are out to win and some will do whatever it takes, no matter how unethical. Some attorneys are so determined to win for their client that they will lie to judges and fabricate circumstantial evidence to make an innocent person appear quite guilty. A classic example of this tactic occurs in rape cases where the defense attorney for the accused interrogates the victim in such a way that she is made to look like a culprit. "Everything you say can and will be used against you."

In the case of Harold Mead, his public defender made a deal with the prosecution that if Mead confessed to the murders of the three mentally retarded youths, authorities would not bring him up on charges for any other murders. The prosecutor knew that a confession meant a conviction for three counts of murder and this would put Mead away for life. Thus Mead was never tried for the murders of the other girls; those cases technically remain open and unsolved to this day. The State's Attorney felt that this conviction would place Mead in prison for the rest of his life. What the prosecutor didn't foresee was that the protocol for parole would change. The State eventually released Mead on furloughs until the day the woman was found murdered at the park where Mead and his wife celebrated their wedding anniversary.

Harold Mead is an example of those criminals who make it to incarceration, only to be released way before their sentence should have expired. John Rice is an example of an individual who went through the system for murder and who should have remained many years in an insane asylum, yet the State released him into society. In many ways, the system does not work and does not guarantee justice. Its problems are too complex and it is run by human beings who make mistakes and bad decisions every day.

According to criminal profiler Greg Cooper, "The system is light years ahead of what it once was." He added that "this cannot prevent an obsessed person from achieving their obsessions. We can try to reroute them and we do that through direct police intervention, forced counseling, and other programs, but if you can kill the president you can kill anybody."

Thus, the main solution to the problem of unsolved crime rests with the individual. Each of us must take responsibility for our own safety and for the safety of our children. Many of the children who are abducted are taken while they are very close to home, and they all have one thing in common: they were all out of their parents' sight and were unattended at the moment they were abducted. Many criminals do not set out to commit a crime, nor do they hunt for victims. Though this does occur, the majority of criminals commit crimes because the opportunity presents itself.

In one case, a mother and her five-year-old daughter were at church and the little girl took a walk to go to the bathroom. While she was alone in the hall, an older man with criminal tendencies happened to walk in. When he found the young girl alone, he kidnapped and murdered her. He had never committed a murder before in his life – but the opportunity presented itself.

Some of the true accounts of child abductions are shocking and reveal how easy it is for someone to abduct a child. One nine-year-old girl was abducted only 20 feet from where her father was standing. In Virginia, a serial murderer abducted two sisters from their porch. Their bodies were found several days later. Sadly, many of the stories read the same way: the child leaves the parents' sight for only minutes, but is gone forever.

Killers will even go into a home to abduct a child. A California woman happened to walk in on someone who was trying to lead her child out of the house. She discovered that the perpetrator had killed two other children only a short time before.

Mary Mount played in a park that was located just behind her home. She played there many times and arrived home safe each time. Unlike inner-city communities, New Canaan boasted a relatively low crime rate during an era where child abductions were virtually unheard of. Mary Mount was alone for only 10 minutes, and in those 10 minutes the wrong person entered the area, saw an opportunity he couldn't resist, and ended Mary's life that day.

The police cannot be everywhere; there isn't enough funding. The responsibility lies with parents to make sure they keep their children within their sight at all times. Most parents feel that once their children reach 10 to 12 years of age, it's okay to give them more freedom. Children in their preteen years, however, are very popular targets for pedophiles, and many children in this age group are abducted because at this age they are allowed out alone.

The responsibility lies with the parents and with each of us for our own safety. Some people refuse to live in fear or worry, and believe that these crimes happen to "other people." Joseph and Lily Mount never imagined that this would happen to them. When they moved to New Canaan, they followed in the footsteps of many executives who transferred there before them and many who have transferred there since. Yet, just as this tragedy happened to them, it could happen to anyone.

For those of us who lived during that time, Mary Mount became a lesson to us all; a lesson that no place offers complete safety. After the Mounts left town, Sid Greenberg, the town newspaper's photographer, along with Phil Blasius, a police officer, made it their mission to look after Mary's grave. Anonymous residents would regularly plant flowers at various times of the year. Phil Blasius donated his entire pension to have flowers placed on

Mary's grave once a year until the funds ran out. Although Mary Mount might have been a mother herself today, she forever remains a 10-year-old girl with a big smile.

On top of the hill at the Rice's graves rests a solitary flag. No one plants any flowers or looks after the graves of Edith, Janet, Stephen, or Nancy. A large stone that bears only the name RICE stands over a plot of land, under which rest the coffins of John Rice, Jr.'s family. The stone does not bear the first names or birth and death dates of the individual victims as if, in their burial, John Rice, Sr. chose to keep his family's horrific end private. Placing a typical tombstone with the names and birth and death dates of his family members might have acted as a painful a reminder for Mr. Rice. With the media attention at the time Mr. Rice's protected his family by the omission of the details. Prior to Mr. Rice placing the large stone, small individual plaques bore the names of each family member with their year of death being the same. Young teenagers who went to the seminary with friends shrieked in horror when they came across their graves. Mr. Rice changed this when he placed the solitary tombstone that bore the name RICE.

When Mary Mount left her home the fateful day of May 27, 1969, she assumed that a safe, familiar world stood before her. She looked forward to going home for dinner after playing at the sandpile. As Mary began to walk home, she couldn't have imagined the lurking stranger who would take her life. She may have seen him, become frightened by him and decided it was time to go home and to go quickly.

As Criminal Profiler Greg Cooper theorized, when Mary started to walk home, the stranger grabbed her from behind, simultaneously covering her mouth to muffle her screams. In that split second she struggled, knowing that this signaled danger and a serious threat to her life. The man threw her into the front seat of his car. Her struggling and screaming for her life overwhelmed this man and, to quiet Mary, he grabbed an object and with it struck a blow to her head, breaking through her skull and causing immediate brain injury and death.

The killer knew he had to get rid of her body and, being an outdoorsman, he knew of several places. He drove to the best and closest location he could think of to discard the girl and hide his crime. He traveled across the road that divides the Wilton Reservoir and parked his car. The killer made sure no one was around, then picked up the girl's lifeless body and carried her into the woods. He walked along the water's edge on a makeshift path used by fishermen. When the killer felt that he had crossed enough distance from the road, he walked 48 feet from the water's edge into the brush, placed the body in a small clearing, and hurried back to his car.

That night, as Mary's body rested on the moist, dark, earth, Joseph and Lily Mount were facing their worst fears.

One year after the discovery of Mary's body, the Mounts moved out of New Canaan. The boys went onto achieve all of the things Dr. and Mrs. Mount hoped they would attain. Joseph and David, like their father, work in research and computers. Billy is an architect. Joseph Mount eventually died. The gaping hole in his heart that never healed since Mary's death could cause him no more distress.

Many of the townspeople who lived in New Canaan in 1969 have since moved away. The current residents who have small children take them to Kiwanis Park to play and swim. Despite the laughter and sounds of little ones at play, at the back of the park where Mary's killer abducted her, there lingers a chilling silence. Within the area where the sandpile stood in 1969, a silent, invisible memorial stands to a young girl playing in the sand. Over the patch of land where her helpless body lay murdered, and over the grave that is her final resting place, the wind cries, *Mary*.

EPILOGUE

There exists no sadder experience for a parent than the abduction and murder of one of their children. When we hear these stories in the news, we feel the pain for the involved families but, although we can be sympathetic, one can never truly imagine the extent of the horrific pain and grief experienced by those who have lost a child in this manner.

In researching this book, the hardest moments came when I needed to contact families who had experienced the grief that resulted from the murder or abduction of one of their children. Each family handles this tremendous pain differently. Each looks for some kind of an answer as to who would have committed such an act and why. Many of these families never have closure. For the Mounts, the pain is so difficult that to this day they are reluctant to discuss any of the events of 1969. Diane Toney's family would never acknowledge that the body discovered was hers. In their grief, they could not accept her death and would never let go of the hope that she might still be alive. Sadly, it was the police department who, over a decade later, buried Diane's body. They didn't step in because her own family did not care, but rather because her own family's grief and shock was so great, they refused to believe the deceased little girl was theirs.

David Altimari, a reporter for the *Hartford Courant*, recounted to me how Dawn Cave's sister still carries a photo of Dawn to this day. She told David that she had gotten into a fight with Dawn and it was because of that fight that Dawn left the house – to take a walk and calm down. While on that walk, she was abducted.

I think of Holly Piiranian's mother, and I can still hear her voice welling up with tears as she told me that her greatest regret is that she never got to say goodbye.

Lastly I think of Magdeline and John Bish, whose daughter Molly was abducted June 27, 2000 and who wasn't found until three years later in June of 2003. I could hear the tremendous pain in Mrs. Bish's voice as she told me of their tireless efforts to find Molly and her abductor. In desperation, they succumbed to the leads offered by several psychics, which led to only heartbreaking possibilities with no real leads. I can still hear John Bish tell me of the difficulty of having to go and get Molly's coat and other belongings that had been left at the park that day. I can hear how Magdeline Bish's voice instantly brightened when she spoke of how proud she was of the person Molly had become. Mrs. Bish teaches the mentally challenged and she spoke of how Molly loved to work with these children. When Magdeline Bish spoke of her affection for these disadvantaged children, she would for a moment forget her own grief and I could only sit in awe at the strength within her, strength that she didn't realize she possessed. She says night time is the worst because she imagines horrible scenarios that Molly might have found as her fate.

Mrs. Bish told me about a woman from Arizona who contacted her, whose daughter went out for ice cream two years ago and never returned. That woman heard of Molly's disappearance and phoned the family in an effort to talk to someone else who had suffered the same terrible tragedy as herself. Mrs. Bish seemed comforted to know that she was not alone.

None of us can truly imagine the grief. Somehow, when we see a photo or hear a story, we sympathize, but the photo and the story leave out so many important details: the child's personality, the lives that child's presence enriched. No one sees the real pain, the lives that will never be the same, the hearts that will forever remain broken, and the pain that each of the parents will suffer until their own deaths.

I must acknowledge those giants whom I have been honored to both meet and speak with on the phone in the course of researching this book. Greg Cooper, who it has been both my honor and pleasure to know, doesn't view his profession as a job but as a way to make a difference. I think of how Greg Cooper has donated his skills to some police departments who could not afford his services, just to solve a case and get a killer off the streets.

I think of the wonderful police and state police officers who care. Lieutenant Ralph Scott, who worked the Mary Mount and John Rice cases, who later went on to become New Canaan's Chief of Police. Also Sheriff Mike Prozzo, who worked the Connecticut Valley River murders, and how he still lives with the hope that the murderer will be found. I think of Lieutenant Jose Gonsalves, the chief investigator of the New Bedford serial murders, who continues to hope that the case will be solved. I also think of Lieutenant Bob White of the New Haven Police Department, one of the detectives in the Harold Mead case.

The system will most likely never be perfect enough to catch all of the perpetrators of child murders and keep them off of the streets. It will continue to evolve over time, but it will never completely succeed in eradicating these crimes. But, there is great comfort in knowing that with the existence of the individuals that I mentioned and those who are like them, we can be inspired and uplifted by their actions and focus on the good in the midst of such evil.

The Wind Cries Mary

PHOTOS

Kiwanis Park is where Mary's abduction and possibly murder took place. Mary last played at a giant sand pile toward back of the pool which had been drained.

The caretakers home to the right of the pool. His wife and daughter saw the man in the white car.

The sign to the left of the pond where Mary's kitten was found walking.

The sign the killer drove past to get to the sand pile where he could see Mary playing by herself. From the back of Kiwanis the killer had a clear view of pond.

The road taken to the wooded area where Mary's body was placed. The woods in this area are thick and remote. This location is exactly 6 miles from the Kiwanis Park.

Photo of Mary Mount's Grave at Lakeview Cemetery

Photo of Rice Grave for Nancy, Stephen and Mrs. Rice at Lakeview Cemetery

Recent photo of Rice house which is now occupied by another owner.
Photos by© Marcelle Nicolette

Photo of John Rice Jr.

Stephen Rice

Nancy Rice

Mary Mount

Rice and Mount Photos courtesy of The New Canaan Advertiser

BIBLIOGRAPHY

Newspaper Articles:

"F.B.I. Joins Hunt For Missing Girl," *The New York Times*, May 29, 1969

"Father In Appeal For Girl's Return," *The New York Times*, May 30, 1969

"New Canaan Search Pressed For Girl," *The New York Times*, May 31, 1969

"Parents of Missing Girl, 10 Offer Reward In Connecticut," *The New York Times*, June 6, 1969

"Computers Are Brought Into Search for Mount Girl," *The New York Times*, June 14, 1969

"Body Matching The Description of Mary Mount Found by Boys," *The New York Times,* June 18, 1969

"Body Identified As Mary Mounts," *The New York Times*, June 19, 1969

"Reward In Connecticut Killing," *The New York Times*, July 4, 1969

"$50,000 Reward Extended In Slaying Of Mary Mount," *The New York Times*

"4 In New Canaan Family Slain; Alarm Out For Son, 18, and Car," *The New York Times,* December 11, 1970

Paul L. Montgomery, "Hunt Pressed In New Canaan Killings," *The New York Times,* December 12, 1970

"New Canaan Youth Charged In Deaths of 4 In His Family," *The New York Times,* December 13, 1970

"Son Sought In Slaying of Family Surrenders To Arkansas Police," *The New York Times,* December 15, 1970

"Youth Back In New Canaan To Face Murder Charges," *The New York Times*, December 17, 1970

"FBI, New Canaan Police Hunt for Missing Girl," *The Norwalk Hour,* May 28, 1969

"Father Makes Plea For Girl, "Let us know if She's Alive," *The Norwalk Hour*, May 29, 1969

"Housewife Tells It: A Girl, Her Kitten, Then Nothing," *The Norwalk Hour,"* May 29, 1969

"Hope Fades For Mary," *The Norwalk Hour,* May 31, 1969

"Search For Mary Again Fails," *The Norwalk Hour*, June 2, 1969

"PD Sifts All Reports On Mary's Whereabouts," *The Norwalk Hour,* June 3, 1969

"Another Search—Scouts Hunt For Mary Mount," *The Norwalk Hour*, June 4, 1969

"Search For Missing Girl Turns To Norwalk," *The Norwalk Hour*, June 7, 1969

"Find No Clues In Huge Search For Little Mary," *The Norwalk Hour*, June 8, 1969

"Awaiting a Call—Mount Family Lives By Telephone Day and Night," *The Norwalk Hour*, June 10, 1969

"Computer Seeks Mary Mount," *The Norwalk Hour*, June 13, 1969

"Search For Mary In Wilton Woods Proves Negative," *The Norwalk Hour*, June 16, 1969

"Mary Mount's Funeral Held; Probe Goes On," *The Norwalk Hour*, June 20, 1969

"No Claim Made For Rewards In Mount Case," *The Norwalk Hour*, June 21, 1969

"See No Connection—Man Questioned In Mount Case," *The Norwalk Hour*, June 23, 1969

"Missing Girl's Body Found Near Reservoir In Wilton," *The Norwalk Hour*, June 18, 1969

"At Mount Home—Grief Replaces Anxiety," *The Norwalk Hour*, June 18, 1969

"Police Believe Mary's Killer Knew Isolated Death Scene," *The Norwalk Hour*, June 19, 1969

"Many Offers Of Help—Callers Flood New Canaan PD," *The Norwalk Hour*, June 19, 1969

"Scholarship Set Up As Mary's Memorial," *The Norwalk Hour*, June 19, 1969

"Norwalk Man, Postal Worker Booked For 5 Parkway Killings," *The Norwalk Hour*, March 17, 1972

"Stamford Murder Victim Identified," *The Norwalk Hour*, March 17, 1972

Charles R. Mitchell, "Police, Mum Regarding Investigation, Are 'Confident' Miller is Right Man," *The Norwalk Hour*, March 18, 1972

Francis X. Fay Jr. "Rarely Seen In Neighborhood- Self-Styled 'Preacher' Lived Will-O-Wisp Life," *The Norwalk Hour*, March 18, 1972

"Letters To Local Woman Sent By Murder Suspect," *The Norwalk Hour*, March 18, 1972

"Four Slain; Son Missing," *The Norwalk Hour*, December 11, 1970

"Report No Break In Hunt For Rice," *The Norwalk Hour*, December 12, 1970

'John Not A Murderer,' Say Friends," *The Norwalk Hour*, December 12, 1970

"Murder Warrant Issued In New Canaan Slayings," *The Norwalk Hour*, December 12, 1970

"Police Question Murder Suspect As Four In Family Are Buried," *The Norwalk Hour*, December 15, 1970

"Subdued Rice Arraigned, Case Comes Up," *The Norwalk Hour*, December 24, 1970

"Murder Suspect Due Back In New Canaan Today," *The Norwalk Hour*, December 16, 1970

"Bench Warrant Issued For Murder Suspect," *The Norwalk Hour*, December 18, 1970

"Grand Jury Meets Today In Rice Case," *The Norwalk Hour*, January 5, 1971

The Wind Cries Mary

Francis X. Fay Jr., "Policeman Tells of Bloody Scene AT Rice Home," *The Norwalk Hour,* April 18, 1970

Francis X. Fay. Jr., "Expert Testimony Ends Rice Trial On 2nd Day," *The Norwalk Hour,* April 19, 1972

"Court Review Slated—Physicians Take Charge Of Rice," *The Norwalk Hour,* April 20, 1970

"10-Year-Old Girl Lost; All-Night Search Fails," *The New Canaan Advertiser,* May 28, 1969

"Police Hope For New Lead On Lost Girl," *The New Canaan Advertiser,* May 28, 1969

"Mystery Scene—Police Press Search For Mary," *The New Canaan Advertiser,* June 5, 1969

"Mary Mount's Body Found: Killer Hunted By Police: Wide Search Ends In Wilton Woods," *The New Canaan Advertise* , June, 19, 1969

"Questions on Reward Unanswered," *The New Canaan Advertiser,* June 19, 1969

"Doubt Ends With Grief; "Love" Cited," *The New Canaan Advertiser,*

"Police Probe Widens In Mary Mount Case, The Case of Mary Mount," *The New Canaan Advertiser*, June 19, 1969

"$50,000. Reward Posted For Mary Mount's Killer," *The New Canaan Advertiser,* July 2, 1969

"Police Checking Leads After $50,000 Reward," *The New Canaan Advertiser,* July 10, 1969

"$50, 000 Reward Open For Mary Mount Killer," *The New Canaan Advertiser*, August 7, 1969

Anthony P Vitale and John Kovach, "Unsolved Murder Case From 1969 Thrust Back Into the Spotlight," *The New Canaan Advertiser,* April 13, 2000

Nancy Robinson "Lines Being Drawn In School Redistricting Battle," Thursday, *The New Canaan Advertiser,* April 12, 2000

"Can't Remember Anything," Suspected Slayer Tells Police, Four in Family Murdered, "Bodies Discovered By Father, Continued Probe Awaits Return Plane From Arkansas," *The New Canaan Advertiser,* December-16-1970

"Scout Was Source of Mother's Pride," *The New Canaan Advertiser,* December 16, 1970

"Mary Mount Link Termed "Remote" *The New Canaan Advertiser,* December 16, 1970

"Rice Facing Grand Jury On Charge Of Murder," *The New Canaan Advertiser,* December 23, 1970

"Rice Gets Lawyer From Panther Trial," *The New Canaan Advertiser,* December 29, 1970

"Court Asked To Drop Case Against Rice," *The New Canaan Advertiser*, February 4, 1971

Dean Hadley "Rice Inherits $60,000 from Victim's Estates," *The New Canaan Advertiser,* April 27, 1972

"Teen Slayer Committed to Hospital," *The New Canaan Advertiser,* June 22, 1972

"Rice Served 5 1/2 Years, Freed Killer Not Coming Back," *The New Canaan Advertiser,* January 5, 1978

"New Canaan Girl Missing, Police, FBI Suspect Kidnap, Officials Fear Abduction After Futile Searches," *The Stamford Advocate,* May 28, 1969

"Missing Girl's Father Appeals For Information, Her Safe Return," *The Stamford Advocate,* May 29, 1969

"Police, FBI Visit Neighbors In Hunt For Missing Girl," 10, *The Stamford Advocate,* May 31, 1969

"New Canaan Police Ask Search of Woods," *The Stamford Advocate,* June 2, 1969

"New Search Launched For Mount Girl Clues," *The Stamford Advocate,* June 3, 1969

"Boy Scouts Searching For Missing Girl," *The Stamford Advocate,* June 4, 1969

"$15,000 REWARD," *The Stamford Advocate,* June 7, 1969

"Mary Mount's Body Found In Wilton: Dental Charts Study Confirms Identity," *The Stamford Advocate,* June 18, 1969

"$50,000 Reward Posted For Mount Murder Clues," *The Stamford Advocate,* July 3, 1969

"Police, FBI Redouble Efforts To Find Mary Mount's Killer: Search Centers On Only "Clue—The White Car," *The Stamford Advocate,* June 19, 1969

"Employers In Area Asked To Help In Girl's Death Probe," *The Stamford Advocate,* June 19, 1969

"Private Funeral Services Held For Mary Mount," *The Stamford Advocate,* June 20, 1969

"Doubts Raised About Reward In Mount Case," *The Stamford Advocate,* June 21, 1969

"New Canaan Police Press Kidnap Hunt In Child's Killing," *The Stamford Advocate,* June 24, 1969

"New Canaan Police Chief Finds No Link In Mount Case And Body Of Bethany Girl "Found In Field," *The Stamford Advocate,* July, 2, 1969

"$50,000 Reward renewed," *The Stamford Advocate,* August 8, 1969

"Beware The White Car! School Officials Warn," *The Stamford Advocate,* November 27, 1970

"Miller-Mount Link Probed, Beth Barlow," *The Stamford Advocate,* April 21, 1972

"Judge Opens New Canaan Files," *The Stamford Advocate,* October 7, 1977

"Police Review Mary Mount Murder Case," *The Stamford Advocate,* April 27, 1978

Nick Seminoff "Four Brutally Murdered In New Canaan: Hunt Honor Roll Boy In Family Killing," *The Stamford Advocate,* December 11, 1970

"Authorities Continue Manhunt In Gory New Canaan Murders," *The Stamford Advocate,* December 12, 1970

"Students Say They Saw Car; Police Searching Campsites," *The Stamford Advocate,* December 12, 1970

Dean Hadley "Youth Described As Quiet Loner," *The Stamford Advocate,* December 11, 1970

The Wind Cries Mary

Nick Seminoff "Rice Murder Warrant Issued As Search For Youth Widens," *The Stamford Advocate,* December 14, 1970

"Murder Suspect Surrenders To Authorities In Arkansas," New Canaan Police Go To "Pick Up Rice Youth," *The Stamford Advocate.* December 15, 1970

"Rice Returning To New Canaan To Face Murder Arraignment," *The Stamford Advocate,* December 16, 1970

Elain Jarvick, Nick Seminoff, "Rice Returned Under Guard: Court Arraignment Postponed," *The Stamford Advocate,* December 17, 1970

"Rice Murder Charge Speeded To Higher Court For Action," *The Stamford Advocate,* December 22, 1970

"Jan. Grand Jury Date For New Canaan Youth," *The Stamford Advocate,* December 22, 1970

"Black Panther Co-Council Koskoff Will Defend Rice," *The Stamford Advocate,* December 23, 1970

"Constitutional Rights, Rice Hearing" *The Stamford Advocate,* January 29, 1970

"Grand Jury Date Is Set For Rice," *The Stamford Advocate* ,January 29, 1971

"Judge Nixes Rice's Attempt For Juvenile Court Transfer," *The Stamford Advocate,* July 16, 1971

"Teeth Impressions Of Rice Evidence," *The Stamford Advocate,* February 5, 1972

"Rice Acquitted In Murder: Judge Panel Cites 'Insanity' *The Stamford Advocate,* April 19, 1972

"Rice Judged Insane Felt "Urge To Kill" *The Stamford Advocate,* April 20, 1972

"Urge To Kill Motivated Rice, Don Ross," *The Stamford Advocate* ,April 20, 1972

"Young Rice Inherits Victims' $60,000," *The Stamford Advocate,* April 28, 1972

"Court Rules Rice III, Committed to Hospital," *The Stamford Advocate,* June 21, 1972

"Judge Backs Release of Rice NC Ax Slayer," *The Stamford Advocate,* December 29, 1977

Deborah Disesa "Town Outraged That A 'Killer' Walks Free, *The Stamford Advocate,* December 30, 1977

Tom Wallace "The Price of Killing," *The Stamford Advocate,* January 3, 1978

Nancy Hendrick "Hope Fades For Mary: Kidnapped Girl Feared Dead," *Connecticut Herald,* June 1, 1969

Nancy Hendrick "Police Check Lead In Mary Mystery," *Connecticut Herald,* June 1, 1969

"Did Slayer Of 4 Kill Mary Mount," *Connecticut Herald,* December 13, 1970

Harry Neigher "Sidelights To New Canaan Murders, Behind The Blood Bath," *Connecticut Herald,* December 13, 1970

"Police Check New Lead In Mary Mount Murder, Police Seek Molester," Neighbor, *Connecticut Herald,* July 12, 1970

Lee, Evelyn "Townspeople Asked To Aid In Child Hunt," *Bridgeport Sunday Post,* June 1, 1969

Lee, Evelyn "Simple Ceremony Ends Mary Mount Tragedy," *Bridgeport Sunday Post.* June 22, 1969

Carl J. Pelleck, Steven Marcus "Dad In Plea For Missing Girl, 10," *The New York Post*, May 29, 1969

Dick Belsky "Hunt Son in Connecticut Slayings," *The New York Post,* December 11, 1970

"Quiet Desperation Follows The Search For Little Mary," *New York Daily News,* June, 2, 1969

"Dad Finds Wife& 3 Butchered; Hunt a Son," *New York Daily News,* John Murphy

"Computers Seek Girl," *UPI*

"Wilton Search For Mary Mount To Start Sunday Morning at 9," *Wilton Bulletin,* June 11, 1969

Dave Altimari and Jane E. Dee, "Suspicions Swirl In Death At Beach: Two Inmates Implicate Convicted Murderer Meade In 1992 Slaying," *Hartford Courant*, April 4, 2000

Dave Altimari, Colin Poitras and Jane Dee, "Four Deaths: A Trail Left Cold," *Hartford Courant*, April 2, 2000

Stephen Fuzesi Jr "Police Hope Murders Won't Hit 1969 Impasse," *New Haven Register,* August 14, 1970

"Psychiatrists Links Recent Slayings To Three Others," *New Haven Register,* August 19, 1970

Gary J. McTrottes "Ahern: Psychiatrist Links Five Slayings," *New Haven Journal Courier,* August 19, 1960

Karen Jeffrey "Clark Reveals Acts of Torture, Cannibalization To Police," *Cape Cod Times*, January 7, 2000

Katherine Shaver "Clark Defense Rests Without His Testifying," *The Washington Post* , October 15, 1999

Paul Duggan "Prime Suspects: Parts 2-5, The Michele Dorr Story," *The Washington Post Magazine,* August 10, 1997,

Paul Duggan "Prime Suspects Part 11," *The Washington Post Magazine,* August 1997

Eric Williams "Clark Body Hunt Comes Up Empty," *Provincetown Banner,* January 20, 2000

Magazine Articles

Bruce Shapiro photography by Virginia Blaisdell "Framed," *Connecticut Magazine,* October 1991 pp. 33-33-38, 113-118

Nick Seminoff, "The Massacre In New Canaan's Horror House," *Crime Detective,* March pp.30-33, 41-42

The Wind Cries Mary

Documents

Record of Purchase of Mount Home

Record of Sale of Mount Home

Police Report (New Canaan Police Dept) recording the disappearance –Offense and Investigation into the disappearance of Mary Mount) dated 5/27/69 at 8:25 p.m. Various pages removed by police and small paragraphs blacked out, 107 pages

A drawing of the scene of the abduction, the body with measurements, notations concerning body's position and clothing and a 2nd drawing of the crime scene. 4 pps. Copies submitted to me by Michael Angelostro one of the detectives who worked the case at the time, from his private collection of notes.

Police Report (New Haven Police Dept) Locations of Harold Meade III information. pp. 95,96,158,

Harold Meade Timeline, by Dave Altimari

RECORD OF DEATHS: Edith Janet Rice, Nancy Janet Rice, Stephen Joseph Rice, Edith Fitzpatrick
Death Certificate: Mary Mount
Intestate Certificate (Probate record) for John Rice
Copy of Certificate of Marriage, John Rice and Edith Fitzpatrick

World Wide Web

http://www.wic.org/bio/debakey.htm
Bio of Dr. Michael E. Debakey, M.D.
http:///www.scouting.org/factsheets/02-516.html pp.1-4
http://members.aol.com/_ht_a/kthynoll/myarticle.htm "My article on child violence," (School Youth Statistics) Kathy Noll, pp.1-4
http://www.bullybeware.com/moreinfo.html Bully B'ware-More Information, pp.1-10
http://www.astolat.demon.co.uk/forensic/forpsych.htm, Forensic Psychology pp.1-6
http://www.cslnet.ctstateu.edu/statutes/title54/t54-p7.htm, General Statutes of CT, Revised to 1997 Title-54-Criminal Procedure, pp. 1-8

Books

Philip E. Ginsberg, <u>The Shadow of Death: The Hunt For a Serial Killer</u>, Charles Scribner and Sons, New York, 1993

Eric W. Hickey, <u>Serial Murderers and Their Victims</u>, Second Edition, Wadsworth Publishing Company, California State University Fresno, 1996

Steven A. Egger, <u>The Killers Among Us: An Examination of Serial Murder And its Investigation</u>, Prentice Hall, New Jersey, 1998

John Douglas and Mark Olshaker, <u>Obsession</u>, Simon and Shuster, New York, 1998

John Douglas and Mark Olshaker, <u>Mindhunter</u>, Simon And Shuster, New York, 1995

John Douglas and Mark Olshaker, <u>Journey Into Darkness</u>, Simon and Schuster, New York, 1997

Robert D. Keppel, Ph.D with William J. Birnes, <u>Signature Killers: Interpreting The Calling Card of the Serial Murderer</u>, Simon and Schuster, New York, 1997

Stanton E. Samenow, Ph.D, <u>Inside The Criminal Mind</u>, Random House, New York, 1984

www.ingramcontent.com/pod-product-compliance
Lightning Source LLC
Chambersburg PA
CBHW070549170426
43201CB00012B/1777